D1452659

WITHDRAWN

Margery

THOMAS R. TIETZE

Margery

HARPER & ROW, PUBLISHERS

New York
Evanston
San Francisco
London

Material from "Truth and the Margery Mediumship" by Mark Richardson is quoted with the permission of Marian Nester. Copyright © 1973 by Marian Nester.

Margery.Copyright © 1973 by Thomas R. Tietze. All rights reserved. Printed in the United States of America. No part of this book may be used or reproduced in any manner whatsoever without written permission except in the case of brief quotations embodied in critical articles and reviews. For information address Harper & Row, Publishers, Inc., 10 East 53rd Street, New York, N.Y. 10022. Published simultaneously in Canada by Fitzhenry & Whiteside Limited, Toronto.

FIRST EDITION

Designed by Dorothy Schmiderer

Library of Congress Cataloging in Publication Data

Tietze, Thomas R
  Margery.
  Bibliography: p.
  1. Crandon, Mrs. Mina (Stinson) 2. Psychical research. I. Title.
BF1283.C85T5 1973   133.9'1'0924 [B]   72–11364
ISBN 0–06–368235–3

Dedicated to Stephen K. Dragland

If a life be delayed till interest and envy are at an end, and all motives to calumny or flattery are supressed, we may hope for impartiality, but must expect little intelligence; for the incidents which give excellence to biography are of a volatile and evanescent kind, such as soon escape the memory, and are rarely transmitted by tradition. . . . If the biographer writes from personal knowledge, and makes haste to gratify the publick curiosity, there is danger lest his interest, his fear, his gratitude, or his tenderness, overpower his fidelity, and tempt him to conceal, if not to invent. There are many who think it an act of piety to hide the faults or failings of their friends, even when they can no longer suffer by their detection; we therefore see whole ranks of characters adorned with a uniform panegyrick, and not to be known from one another. . . . If there is a regard due to the memory of the dead, there is yet more respect to be paid to knowledge, to virtue, and to truth.
—Samuel Johnson (*Rambler* No. 60, October 13, 1750)

The author has seen numerous photographs of the ectoplasmic flow from "Margery," and has no hesitation . . . in saying that it is unquestionably genuine, and that the future will justify the medium as against her unreasonable critics.
—Sir Arthur Conan Doyle, 1926

The Margery case will, in time, come to be considered the most ingenious, persistent and fantastic complex of fraud in the history of psychic research.
—Dr. Walter Franklin Prince, 1934

Contents

Acknowledgments

ANYONE WRITING A BOOK falls into the debt of many people, and when the book is his first, an author finds his gratitude for the help rendered him almost inexpressible. Nevertheless, I will attempt to hint at the contribution of the following people, without whom the book could not have been written.

Mrs. Laura A. Dale, editor of the *Journal of the American Society for Psychical Research,* made available to me the files of Walter Franklin Prince, which contained a wealth of information hitherto unpublished. These large file boxes had been left in Mrs. Dale's charge by Mrs. Lydia Allison, who had herself been entrusted with them by Dr. Prince shortly before his death in 1934. These files had been kept carefully locked ever since, according to Dr. Prince's wishes, until it was considered an appropriate time for the "whole story" of the Margery case to be told. If I have come close to telling the whole story, it is only because of Mrs. Dale's contribution of these materials, her enthusiastic help, and her warm personal friendship. I thank Mrs. Dale also for reading the original manuscript and making many valuable suggestions.

Mrs. Marian Nester, editor of the ASPR *Newsletter* and daughter of Dr. Mark Richardson, loaned me her father's unpublished manuscript, "Truth and the Margery Mediumship," which contains a great deal of material sympathetic to Margery and her phenomena. Mrs. Nester also shared with me her own memories of a childhood and adolescence intimately involved with the case.

The late Mrs. Eileen J. Garrett, then president of the Parapsychology Foundation, shared many valuable memories of Margery, as did Dr. J. B. Rhine and Dr. Louisa Rhine, of the Foundation for Research on the Nature of Man, who also read the manuscript and helped me to clarify the relation of the Margery case to modern parapsychology.

I wish to thank Charles Honorton, of the Department of Psychiatry at Maimonides Medical Center in New York, for reading the manuscript in several stages of production and for contributing the introduction; Dr. Mulford Q. Sibley of the Department of Political Science, Mrs. Maeve Beck of the Department of English, both of the University of Minnesota, and Rhea White, librarian for the American Society for Psychical Research, for having read the manuscript and encouraging me to believe in the value of this work; and D. Scott Rogo, who traveled across the country to read my book and make many suggestions stemming from a considerable acquaintance with the literature of mediumship.

I am especially grateful to Martin Ebon, whose faith and persistence alone account for the publication of this book.

Beyond these, I wish to mention the following deeply personal debts of gratitude:

To Justin Oudal, Minneapolis book dealer, who helped me stock my library with many rare volumes on psychical research and who taught me the love of scholarship and the joys of digging for months in old books to find a single fact.

To John Loegering, my teacher, who taught me the art of critical thinking and the significance of searching for the truth, honestly, objectively, and dispassionately; it is to him that I owe the intellectual foundations of my work.

To Patricia Cady and Stephen K. Dragland, who followed the clues of this mystery every step of the way with me in frequent and long discussions over the evidence, and who listened patiently to me as I tried, over and over again, to find the secret behind this intricate case.

To Mrs. Dorothy Tietze and Miss Pat Wheeland, who helped type the manuscript in its revised forms.

To Miss Susan Webster, who is alone responsible for lending me the reserves of strength and energy necessary to undertake four years of research and three years of writing, and who, after typing the much longer original manuscript from over five hundred pages of crabbed handwriting, did me the kindness of marrying me.

I hope that *Margery* lives up to all the faith, encouragement, and friendship offered by all of these people. It is, after all, their book.

Thomas R. Tietze

Introduction

Margery chronicles a perverse but fascinating and important chapter in the history of what we today call parapsychology. Looking back with the advantage of almost half a century, we might be tempted to characterize this period as the Roaring Twenties of psychical research. Spirits of more than one variety were pursued during Prohibition, and some would say to equal effect. Society's official stance toward spirits—be they bottled or disembodied—does not, it would seem, eradicate the desire for them.

In the aftermath of World War I, interest in mediumistic powers and spiritualism reached an all-time high. Influential publications like *Scientific American* offered prizes for the demonstration of genuine psychic phenomena. Writers such as Sir Arthur Conan Doyle, physicists like Sir Oliver Lodge, and other prominent personalities of the day proclaimed that communication with the dead had been successfully achieved. Others, like Houdini, pronounced with equal enthusiasm that all psychical phenomena were fraudulent or otherwise due to normal (i.e., currently understood) principles, and took it as their duty to debunk mediumistic claims. We see in this story the perennial clash between those who would save humanity from materialism and those who would save it from its animistic roots.

The dilemma of mind and matter has plagued philosophers since antiquity. The controversy has been fought on many battlefields, and while present-day science and philosophy have called an armistice, the dilemma remains. Several philosophers of science have pointed to parapsychology as its last battle-ground.[1] There has, however, been inordinate resistance to the development of empirically verifiable approaches in this area. Both believers and disbelievers in the world of spirits and psychic powers have been highly ambivalent toward parapsychology.

Why? To the overly committed—and naïvely uncritical—believer in psychic phenomena, parapsychology is seen as monotonous laboratory studies and dry statistics that can only be regarded as trivial when compared to the "strong" phenomena of the seance-room. To the hypercritical—though often dogmatic—disbeliever, psychical research is ancient superstition packaged for modern consumption by those who have, with minimal cerebration, "taken leave of their senses." The diehard skeptic frequently points to the seance-room fraud as if to cast in doubt the work of the laboratory. This extraordinary mental feat is equivalent to viewing the achievements of modern technology through the products of New Zealand aborigines.

Why is it that parapsychology and the claims it seeks to investigate draw so heavily on the extremes of human credulity and incredulity? The occurence of extrasensory perception and psychokinetic phenomena may have implications that are as important to our understanding of human beings as quasars and pulsars are to the human being's understanding of the cosmos. Little is currently known about either. Parapsychological capacities, like the black holes of space, are mysteries; but being, so to speak, "closer to home," the questions they raise are somewhat more unsettling. They awaken within us long-dormant queries—"How do we come to know what we know?"—and call for a reappraisal of what we have been taught since early childhood to regard as our "self-boundaries." Parapsychology challenges (or is at least perceived to challenge) basic assumptions we make about our own nature, our destiny, and the extent to which our presently constructed view of reality is idiosyncratic.

The story of Margery demonstrates very clearly the futility of attempting to reach sound judgment on the basis of phenomena occurring only with the protection of darkness and loose control. It also dispels the notion of parapsychologists as easily duped miracle-mongers. The most devastating investigations of Margery were those of the professional psychical researchers—William McDougall, Walter Franklin Prince, J. B. Rhine.

But *Margery* is not simply the story of misguided enthusiasts and hopeful debunkers. It symbolizes the transformation of psychical research into parapsychology. The period surrounding the Margery mediumship signaled a transition of major import. One can only guess at the effect exposure to (and of) Margery may have had on the future direction of J. B. Rhine. That he went on to develop a rigorous laboratory approach to the exploration of psychic claims, with unselected individuals rather than special mediums, suggests a possible reaction formation. In the case of others, Hoagland and Boring for instance, the reaction formation was complete. Their original sympathy, even enthusiasm, turned to disenchantment with the witch of Lime Street, and left them both thoroughly disillusioned with psychical research. Much the same may be said of Dingwall, whose disillusioned presence lingers on in English parapsychological circles.

The *Journal of Parapsychology,* founded in 1937 by McDougall and Rhine, is now in its thirty-sixth year of publication. The *Journal of the American Society for Psychical Research,* in its sixty-sixth year, is now capably edited by Mrs. Laura A. Dale, who along with Dr. Gardner Murphy is responsible for saving the ASPR from Margerydom in the early 1940s. Modern parapsychological research facilities, with their electroencephalographs and electronic testing equipment, would seem alien to psychical researchers of the late 1920s and 1930s. If Prince's enchanted boundary has lost some of its charm (and certainly all of its innocence) in the process of maturation, important gains have been made.

Recent studies of ESP and psychokinetic capacities in animals, for example, strengthen the impression formed earlier through experiments with diverse human populations that psi (psychic) ability is widespread. It now seems likely that it is possessed by all higher mammals. Work has even been attempted with unicellular creatures, but with organisms of low mass especially, it becomes moot as to whose psi is responsible—experimenter's or subject's.

Another impression, one more familiar to the psychical researcher of the twenties and early thirties, is that flashes of psi impressions are more prominent in certain altered states of consciousness. Experimentally induced ESP effects in dreams, hypnosis, and other altered states represent work on a different frontier of parapsychology. Current trends indicate that extrasensory effects may be associated with reduction in awareness of our external sensory environment.

Human survival after death is, of course, the final frontier, and one to which parapsychology is returning after many years. Current explorations of out-of-the-body experience, "memories" of previous lives, poltergeist activity, and the expanding boundaries of ESP reflect the broadened base of inquiry. While resolution of the survival problem is not in sight, the confirmation and exploration of psi phenomena converge with technological advances to make eventual resoltuion feasible. Can we, at this stage, ask for more than a feasible approach to mankind's oldest question?

CHARLES HONORTON
Department of Psychiatry
Maimonides Medical Center
Brooklyn, New York

Preface

THIS BOOK IS a study of the extraordinary. Perhaps no other life has been such a perfect union of the human, the angelic, and the diabolical than the life of Mina Stinson Crandon, known as Margery the medium. Stewart Griscom, of the *Boston Herald,* wrote to an official of the American Society for Psychical Research on June 18, 1927, giving the following estimate of the case: "It is profoundly and sardonically humorous . . . with almost a Molière touch. It has mystery, veiled motivations, true tragedy, howling farce, and a pervading aura straight from Alice in Wonderland. Almost everyone who becomes involved shoots off at tangents; respected clergymen and savants suddenly become voluble liars; there are meaningless statements apropos of nothing; logic and normality take extended holidays."

With the newsman's unerring instinct for a good story, Griscom captured the character—the atmosphere—of the Margery mediumship. This book tells the story of that affair, and of its bearing upon the course of psychical research. The mystery, the tragedy, the farce, and the inexplicable motivations are all here, with no serious attempt to supply an answer. I make no pretense of having found one.

The picture painted here, therefore, cannot fail to be unfinished, in spite of the enormous mass of data available to me. Aside from published material dating from 1924 to 1940, I have, through the kindness of Mrs. Laura A. Dale of the American

Society for Psychical Research, made use of Dr. Walter Franklin Prince's confidential correspondence that has never before been made public. Together they make our knowledge of Margery's actions and those of her contemporaries nearly complete. At the same time, it is not enough to know how she behaved—or how she was said to have behaved—in any number of critical situations in her life. We must know things that perhaps only she could tell us, and perhaps even she could not supply the deficiency.

For she lived, not in a panorama, but in a very narrow space; she was lonely, warm, bitter, innocent, raucous, genteel, uncouth, sophisticated. She had practically no sense of the history in which she lived and only a vague suspicion that she was gaining a great deal of heartily welcome attention. She could lie with charm, threaten with innocence, cajole with felicity, and scheme with charity. Her life was a jumble of paradoxes.

No one denies that she was greatly and widely loved, nor that she was also heartily despised. She breathed a bit of life into a dying religion, and at the same time nearly destroyed a scientific discipline of the first importance. She was therefore bound to create both friends and enemies. But it is important to understand beforehand that these friends and enemies are the only ones who wrote the primary data on which any historical account of her life must be based. She was thought to have been a saint by some and a whore by others—there is no height to which her friends have not elevated her; there is no depth to which her enemies have not consigned her.

The necessary result is confusion. She was an enigma in her own time; we cannot expect her to be less in ours. I find Dr. Prince's metaphor strikingly apt: she was a star that burst suddenly into the sky and slowly burnt itself out. And when it was all over, she—like an astronomical event—was recorded by history to have occurred and forgotten by men to have lived.

Much of the charm of any history lies in one's certain knowledge that one can never know anything for certain. The great charm of the Margery case lies in the absence of anyone who pretends to have understood it.

It was an event, an event that is now over and long forgotten. When it is remembered at all, it is remembered imperfectly. From 1925 until her death in 1941, Mina Crandon was known as Margery, the medium. During the twenties, reports of wonders in her seance room were widespread and her name was a byword in American Spiritualism. She was the center of an international set of admirers that included Sir Oliver Lodge, Sir Arthur Conan Doyle, William Butler Yeats, Hamlin Garland, Charles Richet, Gustave Geley, and other prominent men. She was the light around which countless visionaries danced and paid homage; she was, in the words of one acquaintance, "the Queen of psychical research."

Psychical research was a very different thing in her day than it is today. In England, where the scientific study of Spiritualism began, the research interest centered on the so-called mental phenomena known today as extrasensory perception. In France the focus was on activities that the popular mind associates with Spiritualism, that is, the physical phenomena. In America, there was a tendency to enlarge the focus, and consequently to blur the picture. Nonetheless, many American psychical researchers, eminent in other fields and possessed of perceptive analytical intelligence, had established for psychic study a considerable degree of respectability.

The years that followed Margery's fall saw impressive growth in the number of eminent scientists engaged in the study of psychic phenomena; that change was in no little part due to the Margery mediumship.

In the account that follows, we will see Mina Crandon romping and cavorting, creeping and struggling, toward fame.

She was deep and frivolous, superficial and solemn. There is no answer to her life; there can only be a record of it.

But underlying that record will be the ubiquitous, fascinating —and somewhat nettling—question: "What and who was she?" Perhaps we will never know.

But we will certainly always be able to wonder.

I

The Beginning

TOTAL BLACKNESS engulfed the room. Several men and a few women sat silently around a wooden table. All of them—businessmen, lawyers, physicians, and journalists—were careful to hold the hands of the persons next to them. Suddenly a shrill whistle broke the silence and the tension eased.

"Hello, Walter," someone in the circle said. "Where have you been?"

"Oh," replied a voice, "I had to take my girl to a strawberry festival."[1]

Surprise and delight mingled in the laughter that followed, for the jovial voice in the dark was that of a ghost, but "Walter," as he was called, was anything but the popular image of his kind. These twentieth-century people, engaged in the age-old ritual of the seance, had not expected to be amused while attempting to raise the dead. A whimsical, witty, sharp-tongued shade—that was Walter.

"Can you read my mind?" a participant asked.

"Yes, but you wouldn't want me to tell *that!*"

Laughter again, and then someone asked, "Walter, when you are relaxed, do you surround yourself with youth and beauty?"

The ghost laughed heartily and patted the speaker's head. "No," the voice said. "I'm not relaxed when youth and beauty are around. I'm under fifty!"[2]

Then Walter asked if the sitters would like to see a materialization. They all replied in the affirmative.

"Okay," he said. "Here goes!"

There was a moment of silken rustling and then a hoarse voice asking for light. One of the sitters snapped on a handlamp covered with red paint. The crimson glow played upon the table in a vague circle.

Suddenly, from the surrounding darkness, an object slapped limply upon the wood. The sitters leaned forward and studied the object. It was a gray, twisted hand, with its irregular fingers ending in clawlike nails. Knotted with cords resembling muscular tissue, the hideous, inhuman hand twitched once and fell out of sight beneath the table.

A moment later the room lights went on. Everyone rubbed his eyes, adjusting to the sudden change. Only one woman remained quietly seated, her eyes closed. The man at her right touched her shoulder gently and her eyelids fluttered. Then she smiled and asked how the seance had gone. She had, it seems, been in trance.

Everyone assured her that the sitting had been a dramatic success—another proof of the reality of supernormal occurrences by the incredible Margery the medium.

Mina Stinson was born in 1888 on a farm in Princeton, Ontario, not far from Toronto.[3] We know little about her life except that it was dominated by her father's grim philosophy and harsh demands, which his wife's warmth and forebearance softened only slightly. Loving, patient and pliable, Mother Stinson continued to influence her daughter's life into her declining years. But it was Mina's brother, Walter, five years her senior, who was her real consolation. A strong and strapping youth, Walter managed to avoid the rigorous nature of his father's religious obsession and to retain the individual spirit and compelling sense of humor that would be his most consistent characteristic. Walter was the family rebel, the only one strong enough to break with family patterns. Warm, open, cheerful and friendly, he always called Mina "The Kid."

Mina needed the love and friendship that Walter provided.[4] He made her long days light and happy with scandalous tales of his adventures, some of which were true.

The two youngsters shared bonds of sympathy as well. A close friend was their elderly cousin, Henry McNeeley. Within his twisted body, deformed and crippled by an accident in his youth, there dwelt mysterious powers that were Mina's first recorded experience with psychic phenomena. Henry was a dowser, one of those individuals who claimed to be able to find water and minerals through the twitchings of a forked stick—and a little clairvoyance. Although nearly infallible, he had to bear the unkindness and ridicule of the ignorant. All the wells on the Stinson farm had been dug at Henry's command, and Mina and Walter listened with fascination as he told of his inexplicable ability.[5]

A few other facts filter down from Mina's childhood: the great affection she felt for their dog Victor,[6] and the story of Walter impulsively giving away his expensive overcoat to a tramp while on an excursion to the city.[7] Their insignificance only points out our ignorance of these important years.

One fragment that has import is the alleged psychic ability of Walter during his life. During the Margery years, supporters would claim that Walter "produced with tables action so violent that the tables were completely demolished,"[8] and that "during his life he was credited with psychic powers."[9] The enigmatic Dr. Crandon, Margery's husband, would write: "In his youth Walter Stinson had tables tilt and levitate, in his presence, in daylight. This was looked on as a diversion and never taken seriously."[10] When later accounts deduced from the statement that Walter was a medium, Crandon never took issue. Attempting to establish a rationale behind Walter's "return," Crandon felt it would add credibility to the claim to suggest that Walter had been a medium himself. Much of the literature of the Margery case is characterized by the same kind of snowballing implicational error.

Mina herself divulged the probable truth of the matter in a very entertaining interview she gave in 1926. During her childhood, she explained, nothing was farther from her thoughts than spiritism. Her first real exposure was Walter's account of a seance he had attended during a trip to Boston. Returning, he told everyone about his curious visit to the big-city medium, and teased the children into delight and terror with his "spook-show" tricks. He may have been moving a table by way of demonstration, probably with his foot, as a joke. The sense of humor characteristic of Walter's later "personality" must have enhanced the "supernormal" event.[11]

The table-tipping adventures ended when Mr. Stinson forbade all mention of the heathen practices of Spiritualism.[12] Mina may have even appreciated her father's strictures because she was more frightened than amused by Walter's demonstrations.

Eventually the Stinsons diversified. Walter led the independence movement by working on the railroad, putting his brawny shoulders to good use, but relaxing his clever wit.[13] Many years later Mina told a story of the intellectual capabilities upon which Walter turned his back. She recalled that he had been a mathematical prodigy, capable of adding long columns of figures with incredible swiftness. This ability was then popularly thought to be a psychic capacity. Of course we know nothing of the truth of the tale.

Following Walter's exodus, Mina too pulled up stakes at the age of seventeen, having completed her secondary schooling "with good standing."[14] Boston, the "hub of the universe," to which she moved in 1904, would be her home for the rest of her life.

She obtained employment as secretary of the Union Congregational Church, under the pastorate of the Reverend Allen A. Stockdale. Now the saucy independence that marked her personality first became apparent.[15]

The documentation of these years is infuriatingly sparse. City records state that she was married on September 5, 1910, to Earl P. Rand.

Mina was very fond of music and practiced for hours on the cello. She was quite accomplished at the instrument and derived a great deal of pleasure from playing in the church orchestra.[16] She also enjoyed the cornet and the piano, as well as local amateur theatrics.

Then, in 1911, the most significant event in her life occurred. A boxcar overturned and crushed Walter. He survived the accident for three hours, his strength of will serving to hold off the inevitable, and then he was dead, at the age of twenty-eight.

This tragic event was to have profound effects on Mina's nature, but they would not emerge for several years.

Mina continued to occupy herself with music and with her church. Two years after Walter's death, her son John was born, giving her great consolation and an outlet for her characteristically affectionate nature. Contemporary gossip claimed that John's birth resulted in a sudden discontent and a strong desire to rise above her station as the wife of a small-time grocer in Faneuil Hall.[17] Nonetheless, she and her husband lived contentedly for four more years.

The *Boston Herald* (December 20, 1924) informs us that the marriage suffered its first serious blow in November 1917. Earlier that year, Mina had been hospitalized in Dorchester and operated on by Dr. Le Roi Goddard Crandon, a tall, sophisticated Boston surgeon whose success with women was rumored to be great. There is no evidence that the quarrels in the Rand home were related to Mina's new-found friend, but relations became more and more strained until Christmas Day 1917, the day Mina left Rand's home and went to her mother's place in Belmont. "On January 18, 1918, Mrs. Rand filed her suit for divorce. She charged her husband with cruel and abusive treatment. . . . Rand says that during that period he was dazed. He constantly thought of the future of his boy, who was then five years old. After much hesitation he finally decided that, for the good of all concerned, he would not contest the action. Mrs. Rand petitioned for the custody of the boy."

With the coming of the World War, Mina exercised her independence by volunteering to drive ambulances for a navy hospital, using the wages as a much-needed supplement to her income.[18] It was there that she renewed her acquaintance with Crandon, now the lieutenant-commander who had organized and was directing the special medical unit.

Mina's divorce was granted in March 1918, and became final in September. Rand told reporters that Mina married Crandon very shortly after the divorce was made final. The *Herald* reported: "Rand speaks with calmness of his former wife and of Dr. Crandon. . . . The Crandons buy their groceries from Rand."

A new era in Mina's life was beginning. The scene was set for the most bizarre affair in the history of psychical research.

II

Life at Lime Street

By 1917, Mina had become an attractive and vivacious woman. She was contagiously alive and affecting in her humor as well as in her few recorded depressions.

Humor has been called the essence of her personality. Friends who remember her today agree that she was an utterly charming woman. It is the only element on which both friends and critics agree. Many continue to cherish affectionate memories for her even in the face of her inimical actions in her later years. She bore a quality of agelessness for many years; critics commented on her charms and friends acknowledged them well into the autumn of her life. In 1918 she was a slim and pretty woman whose roundness of limb and pertness of attitude men found "too attractive for her own good."[1] She dressed well and the fashions of the twenties were good to her. She was blue-eyed, with light brown or blonde hair worn in a bob; she once confided that she wore no pins in it. Photographs show clear, frank eyes, and an expression both saucy and penetrating. Photographs taken when it all began and those taken in the late thirties provide a revealing comparison, for the inward turmoil and constant strain under which she lived are indelibly impressed on those yellowed pictures.

But such possibilities were far from her thoughts when she met Le Roi Goddard Crandon for the second time. A Bostonian, Crandon was one of four offspring of a well-to-do family, raised

in a stern atmosphere of oppositon to the traditional religious
faiths. The rigorous intellectual discipline demanded by his father impressed a seriousness upon him while yet a young man.

He served in the navy for two years as a lieutenant-commander
at the head of a medical station, during which time he met Mina.
From 1903 to 1918 he was an instructor of surgery at Harvard
Medical School.[2] He had written a college textbook entitled *Surgical After-Treatment.*

As a practicing surgeon in Boston, Crandon grew more convinced year by year that the nature of man was to be revealed by
the scalpel. Religion, in both its organized and private forms,
became repugnant to him; superstition in any form, and particularly in an advanced society such as his, Crandon hated with the
passion of the most ardent rationalist. "The doctor's favorite
aphorism," it was once observed, was: "You didn't make the
Universe, you must accept it."[3]

A strangely affecting person, the doctor was energetic and
slightly eccentric, a combination that cowed many people into
respect.

As Hamlin Garland observed, when he met Crandon in 1927,
"He was scholarly in appearance, slender, low-voiced, and grace-
ful, entirely in keeping with his book-walled study."[4]

On the surface, one could scarcely imagine a couple with less
in common than the Crandons. Mina's light and happy nature
contrasted strikingly with the doctor's dour personality, and their
religious backgrounds seemed to hinder the relationship from
the beginning. But this history of their relationship indicates that
she was both in love with Crandon and aware of the social standing that he could give her. Which was the more important to her
was and is a matter of dispute, even among her friends.

The answer may lie in a combination of the doctor's impressive
social background and his compelling brilliance. People who
knew him report that he was not well liked at Harvard. He was
coldly self-sufficient and suave; an odd indifference to people,

combined with a powerful intellectual heritage, seemed to make him popular with women and unpopular with his colleagues. It is easy to imagine that Mina was impressed. He represented all the security that she needed so badly.

Crandon was forty-four when he married Mina. He had been married twice before.[5] The *Boston Herald* of December 20, 1924, reports that after the first divorce in 1911, his wife succeeded in retaining custody of their only child and then proceeded to marry one of Dr. Crandon's best friends.

In 1914 he had married Lucy Gill, the divorced wife of an army lieutenant. Apparently this match was even less happy. "In February, 1917, Dr. Crandon filed suit for divorce against the second Mrs. Crandon. The libel was filed in the local superior court. The doctor charged his wife with cruelty and abuse. Many of the specifications in his bill of complaint were sensational."

Whatever the source of their mutual affection, Crandon and Mina married and were at least superficially happy.[6] They made their home where the Back Bay meets Beacon Street, on a road that resembled an alley. The houses fronted directly on the street; generations of building and re-building had made the inharmonious structures blend like stylistic master-pieces in a small museum. The address, which would become synonymous with the mysterious and occult, was Number Ten Lime Street.

It was an old house, four stories high, made warm and complete by Mina's competence as a housekeeper. It became a center of social activity through large, notable and frequent parties. The doctor and his wife became one of the most popular couples in Boston. In these early Prohibition days drinks flowed freely, and friends were made quickly. Mina then possessed an elusive beauty, a delicate and mischievous loveliness. She was glad to be alive, all things were wonderful to her, all people were important. Hers was a mixture of animal beauty and keen feminine perceptiveness; witty, capable and totally charming, Mina Crandon was a woman who could be loved by men and adored by women.

The doctor, by way of contrast, played the host's role with an intellectual urbanity that flattered male guests by addressing their higher capabilities. He was widely read and known to pursue many hobbies. In addition to his fondness for the sea, Crandon was noted for a superb collection of works on Abraham Lincoln; his library was decorated with bronze busts, photographs and rare documents. S. Ralph Harlow, a dubious authority, but a friend of the Crandons at the time, assures us that "he was a respected Lincoln scholar."[7] The Crandon library was also impressively stocked with first editions of Dickens and other valuable rarities.

The doctor's energetic mind had led him in many directions; inevitably he turned to the topic that was on the tongues of so many during the early twenties. Crandon's interest in psychical research began when Sir Oliver Lodge, the famed British physicist, announced his belief in communication with the dead.

Lodge's son, Raymond, had died in the World War; now the esteemed scientist had published the results of his investigations of several spiritualist mediums, among them the great European sensitive, Mrs. Gladys Osborne Leonard. In his book, *Raymond, or Life and Death,* Sir Oliver claimed to have broken the wall between the living and the dead—he had spoken to his still-living son in the eerie darkness of the seance room.

This announcement caused near-pandemonium among contemporary scientists. In common with everyone else, Crandon had been curious about this remarkable conversion, but he had never indulged his curiosity to the point of reading Lodge's books. Then, during a lecture tour through the United States, Sir Oliver stopped in Boston, where Crandon heard for the first time the extraordinary experiences of the great scientist in the shadowy realm of Spiritualism.

Some time later, recalling that evening, he said, "I couldn't understand it. It did not fit into any pattern I had previously known about scientists. So I asked to meet him after his lectures.

We talked for some time that first night. And we met again. We became friends. Sir Oliver suggested some reading for me, and I began, feeling somewhat foolish, but certainly intrigued."[8]

Crandon began his reading in the early months of 1923. Finding nothing that impressed him as conclusive, he was only certain that a good deal remained to be learned. In the spring of that year he began reading the remarkable works of William Jackson Crawford, an Irish engineer and lecturer at Belfast.[9] In them he found a key to the problem of demonstrating psychical phenomena.

It had occurred to him that the mental phenomena studied by Lodge and his associates had always to be evaluated in relation to that old bugbear of parapsychology—chance. The trance utterances of mediums often suggested that the psychic himself had some as yet unknown mental abilities; as evidence for the existence of incorporeal entities, they were not so clear. Chance might be operating, or some obscure mental phenomenon that would one day be traced to an organ beneath the surgeon's scalpel.

But Crawford's experiments with the so-called physical phenomena opened a new line of inquiry for Crandon. If a table tilted, it was a physical fact and not something to estimate in relation to probability. A voice heard in a room where no one was standing was an objective phenomenon and subject to scientific investigation. This was the approach taken by Crawford in his investigation of the Goligher circle.

It had been Crawford's ambitious task to control* an entire family of mediums during a long series of seances in the Goligher home. The conjuring arts were well known to mediums; early investigations had revealed that fraudulent simulations of physical phenomena were used by enterprising mediums. Without a knowledge of the difficult deceptions that mediums used, Craw-

*In psychical research, the verb "control" refers to the holding or fastening of a medium in such a way that will effectively prevent him or her from moving or taking advantage of any opportunity to commit fraud.

ford set out to control not one medium but eight! With the exception of a few isolated but impressive incidents that provide evidence about the case that might warrant a suspended verdict, Crawford usually preferred to work alone.

With the aid of instruments, Crawford verified to his own satisfaction the theory that a psychic substance of unknown composition exuded from the body of the medium when in trance. What the spiritualists called "ectoplasm" was a viscous substance, damp and clammy; often its smell was sickly or unpleasant. Extruding in small portions from the bodily orifices, the ectoplasm took the shapes of hands or faces. In Crawford's experiments, the ectoplasm formed itself into what was termed a "psychic cantilever," since it performed physical work. Photographs of this white, flowing material show it extruding from the medium's lower body and tilting the table. That, the spiritualists had always asserted, was how it was done. Crawford agreed.

Crandon applauded the superficially careful experimentation. But Crawford's work appealed to Crandon in a second, more incisive way. Crawford's critics claimed that he had continually suggested supernormal explanation for the phenomena when a normal explanation was adequate and most obvious. For instance, in many of the experiments, the "psychic cantilever" could as easily have been Miss Goligher's foot. Although this and other objections had been raised before, Crawford could only repeat that he *knew* these people, liked them, and trusted them. They had no possible reason to cheat––the circle was a private one, a religious ceremony, a family affair; why should they cooperate to produce a fraudulent result? No, Crawford asserted, there are facts here that must be assimilated into physics; to ignore them was to close one's eyes to all that science holds highest. The phenomena were genuine; this, Crawford believed, could not be doubted.

One day in 1920 William Jackson Crawford swallowed a deadly poison. Later, a note was found stating that his death had nothing to do with Miss Goligher, her family, or the phenomena they produced. The real reason for his death is a mystery to this day.*

Le Roi Crandon's sympathies were easily swayed by arguments couched in vaguely paranoid terms. Himself something of an underdog when he worked at Harvard, Crandon was often known to utter "vaguely paranoid" things, and his own sense of self-confidence impelled him to trust his judgment on the character of men. Crawford's feelings of unjust persecution were persuasive then and still are: we are made to feel that only bigotry could keep anyone from acknowledging the truth of the experimental findings. In short, Crandon understood and sympathized with Crawford's work.

On a spring evening in 1923, Crandon read far into the night as was his habit. When the last words of Crawford's book had passed through his mind, the doctor gazed up toward the ceiling and closed the volume with slow deliberation.

---

*Basing his conclusions on an examination of certain correspondence pertaining to Crawford's suicide, Mr. D. Scott Rogo, an historian of psychical research, has told me that Crawford had suffered a nervous breakdown as a result of a strenuous and poorly received lecture tour. Mr. Rogo conjectures that Crawford may have killed himself in a moment of lucidity, fearing that the collapse would be total. Mr. Rogo shares the common belief that the breakdown and the resultant suicide were unrelated to the Goligher case.

III

Walter Returns

CRANDON SPENT many long hours reflecting on Crawford's experiments, which came as a jarring note in the seemingly tranquil symphony of a growing scientific materialism. The doctor's nature admitted little that was not amenable to his "fervent rationalism"[1]; some who knew him were surprised at his interest in "spook-hunting." Nearly everyone shared Mina's mystification with her husband's new hobby.[2]

Only Dr. Mark Richardson, an old friend and a new cohort, understood the new interest. Richardson had turned to Spiritualism after a distinguished career in medical research; his fifteen years on the staff of the Massachusetts General Hospital had led to important knowledge of the bacteriology of typhoid fever.[3]

Richardson's mother had been interested in spiritualistic thought; a striking case of poltergeist activity occurred in his home town and was reported in an 1868 *Atlantic Monthly.*[4] But his real interest in metapsychics followed a personal tragedy of the deepest severity.[5] In the summer of 1909 his two young sons, Mark and John, contracted infantile paralysis and died within three weeks.[6]

Stunned by the blow, Richardson and his wife turned to Spiritualism. Sittings with a number of local mediums in Boston convinced the searching couple of the supernormality that formed the basis of all spiritualistic faith.

At this time Richardson and Crandon were both employed as

associate medical examiners for an eastern insurance company.[7] Richardson took it upon himself to enlighten the doctor about Spiritualism and to dissuade him from his materialistic bias.[8]

In a short time, having read the Crawford account, Crandon embraced his colleague's interest with fervor. Within a week, Crandon announced to bewildered friends that he was "intellectually convinced" that the phenomena were genuine. Before long, his name appeared on the membership lists of both the British and American societies for psychical research.[9] Whether or not he truly believed in the reality of psychic phenomena is in doubt even today.

However puzzled, his friends and acquaintances were impressed with Crandon's sincerity. His father often absented himself from Lime Street because he could not bear to hear his son ramble on about ghosts.[10] But Mina reacted quite differently. She listened to her husband's forceful arguments against her religious faith and admitted her own doubts. How could a loving God impose rigid laws, demand abject obedience, or allow hell to exist? Crandon played upon her doubts and his skillful efforts were rewarded. When the doctor announced his conversion to belief in psychical occurrences, it seemed to Mina that he was subscribing to a new religion. In a way, she was right.

Psychical research was then nothing less than the preliminary overture of science toward an attack on the greatest of all empirical problems: the existence of the nonmaterial and its interaction with our world. Many early investigators, delighted by the first bloom of success, enthusiastically supposed that they could reconcile science and religion, acknowledging the reality of religious mysteries and discovering their nature through scientific method.

Crandon bought into a curious position, then, when at last he nodded assent to Richardson's arguments. At first he resisted the frequent invitations to "come along" with his friend to investigate local mediums. During one evening's discussion he revealed to Mina and to Dr. and Mrs. Edison Brown that the most impres-

sive kind of investigation for him would be modeled after Crawford's, in a family circle, each member of which he knew personally. This, Crandon felt, would eliminate considerations of fraud,
for, in a matter of this gravity, no friends could long continue a
hoax without being exposed.

Kitty Brown and Mina laughed about the idea, agreeing to look
in someday on a local clairvoyant, about whom Mrs. Richardson
had told them. On a lark one afternoon, following a session of
horseback riding, Mina and Kitty did stroll rather irreverently
into the psychic's rooms, still wearing their riding clothes. They
had speculated that he would put them off until he could find out
something more about them, or he would indulge them with a
display of mediumistic legerdemain. They expected to be able to
detect any sort of trickery he should try on them.

To their surprise, the clairvoyant not only saw them at once,
but apparently saw through them with ease. Of the many
phenomena presented to them, the most significant for Mina was
an "appearance" by a laughing young man, with broad shoulders
and blond hair. The psychic described this invisible entity for the
ladies, neither of whom was privileged to observe it personally.
From the description, Mina concluded that it was Walter himself
who was trying to break through, to cross that illimitable barrier
between life and death.

Stunned, Mina Crandon sat quietly, awed by the bizarre personality of the man before her. The medium concluded by saying
that she, Mina, had been selected for "The Work," and that she
would be a medium of exceptional—of unparalleled—power. She
must develop her ability . . .

It was all over. It was yet to begin.

The house on Beacon Hill loomed tall and leaned awkwardly
over the narrow street that twenty-seventh of May, 1923, as six
friends gathered within to speak to the dead. It was a singular old
place, well suited for its role. One visitor described it thus:

It possesses an architectural complexity (largely due to extensive remodeling) which surpasses belief. There are two flights of back stairs, affording four independent points of access to the front of the house; there is a butler's pantry with a dumb-waiter. The whole house fairly teems with curious closets, crannies, cubbyholes large and small, blind shaftways, etc., the utility or necessity of which is not always apparent. The more mysterious ones doubtless occupy space that hung heavy on the remodeler's hands, but even when one has formulated this idea some of them are very puzzling.[12]

A house, indeed, poorly suited to disarm one's suspicions, but certainly most characteristic; could one look for a better "haunted house"?

The gathering had mounted the staircase to the fourth floor, to isolate themselves from street noises. The room into which they filed was grim and stuffy, once a den used by Crandon, but recently little occupied. It was eighteen feet one inch by seventeen feet, and its ceiling a full nine feet from the floor.[13] It must have seemed larger, for others would remember it later at six or seven times its actual size, a not unusual tendency in the annals of this case.[14]

On the windows hung chintz curtains; outside, a view of Beacon Hill and a sheer drop of four stories. Bookcases adorned the corners and a part of one wall. In a corner opposite the single door—the only means of entry—reposed a Victrola, its tapering trumpet pouring out the sentimental sweetness of Drdla's "Souvenir." Next to the Victrola was a tapestry brick fireplace and nearby a large sofa. In the course of many years, the furniture would change only slightly, while mementos and gifts would line the shelves of the room, telling, in their mutely voluble way, the story of her life.

They seated themselves at the austere Crawford-table, carefully constructed without nails according to the latest occult instructions, unaware of the gravity of the events that were to follow. Mina was in good humor and had by now dispelled the solemnity that had fallen over her interest in Spiritualism after her visit to that mysterious seer. As she put it, "By this time I was again pretty well unconvinced. But my friends, who had unconvinced me, now became very serious. . . . They were all so solemn about it that I couldn't help laughing. They reproved me severly, and my husband informed me gravely that 'this is a serious matter.' "[15]

They made a circle by linking hands. A faint red glow illuminated the room and played on each of the sitters; according to Crawford and others, the light would allow both visual control and the production of phenomena, for experimentation had shown that psychic structures preferred red light to bright white.

Among the "investigators" were several close friends: the Browns, Frederick Adler, and Alexander Cross. They all concentrated on the table, linking their hands. Next to her, clutching Mina's fingertips, sat Crandon, his face a mask of intense concentration, the light gleaming on his wire-rimmed spectacles.

Suddenly, there was a motion.

Instantly, all attention riveted on the wooden table before them. It slid laterally, very slightly, but perceptibly. Then it rose on two legs and fell to the floor with a crash.

Someone suggested that they attempt to discover which of them was the medium. Crandon urged them to depart from the room one at a time. Kitty Brown arose and left.

The table tilted.

Kitty rejoined the circle, and her husband, Adler, Cross, and then Crandon each left the room in turn. The table continued its curious activity.

When Mina left the room, the table was inanimate. As she reentered at Crandon's call, the sitters greeted her with somewhat awed cheers. Mina, a medium? No one in Boston could have been less likely. Suddenly the idea seemed to be great fun. Nervousness disappeared from the group. Mina Crandon was the heroine of the day.

IV

Knock on Wood

MANY YEARS LATER, when reviewing Driesch's treatise *Psychical Research,* Frederick Bligh Bond included an unquestionable reference to Mina Crandon: "Even a medium of high social position can occasionally be a strange creature, perhaps possessed by an out-of-the-way passion for self-expression, even if not merely by a taste for practical joking."[1]

The continuation of the mediumship may indeed have represented a release for Mina's self-expression. It is a sound assumption that Mina was painfully aware of her intellectual inferiority to her husband; critics of the mediumship have suggested that this accounts for the appearance of the phenomena and their continuation over the years. Some have stated in private conversations that Mina was unsure of her husband's fidelity and was willing to do anything to safeguard her marriage and her son's future.

Even if she were motivated to fraud by such considerations, or by her frivolous sense of humor, Mina was able to produce an extraordinary spectrum of spiritistic phenomena that are very difficult to explain.

The first significant phenomenon was the banal and dubious tilting of the Crandons' table. At the second sitting, a week later, the sitters determined to make a systematic record of the seances and the phenomena produced. Mrs. Richardson was assigned that task. It was at that time that Crandon suggested a code with raps, rather than tiltings, to establish "communication" with the beyond. The table tilted in what was agreed to be an affirmative way, and the agencies ostensibly began to rap on the tabletop. In a short time the raps became strong and a crude code was established.[2] During the year that followed, forty-four discarnate entities would reveal themselves through it.

Gradually, one personality made itself felt more forcefully than the rest; before long, twenty or thirty ghosts relayed their good wishes through this dominant communicator. As the Crandon circle had suspected, the control was none other than Walter Stinson.

Aiding and abetting him were Mark and John, the young sons of Dr. and Mrs. Richardson. The atmosphere of these early sittings was light and far from maudlin. Spiritualists know that death is not the cessation of the personality; everyone was delighted to have established communication with the surviving youngsters.

Another remarkable event occurred at that second sitting. The spirit of Mrs. Caldwell, the mother of Kitty Brown, took control of the table and produced an energetic display of enthusiasm toward Dr. Frederick Caldwell, who was visiting at his sister's invitation. Quoting from the record, "the table followed Caldwell out through the corridor into the bedroom, and forced him upon the bed, rumpling all the mats in transit. Then, on request for more, the table started downstairs after him, when we stopped it to save the wall plaster."[3]

Of this incident only one thing can be said with certainty: it was not Mina's foot that moved it! In the months to follow, the table continued to behave in this curious manner.

There was an air of frivolity in the early days, before truly critical observers began to appear at Lime Sreet. In these carefree days the sitters felt the table vibrating "as though laughing,"[4] the table tilted up on two legs and played a tune on the piano,[5] and a neighbor was dumped on the floor after having decided to sit on the table in an effort to stop its activity.[6]

But it was not only the table that caused wonder at Lime Street. From the seventeenth of June until the fifteenth of November, 1923, the records tell of "psychic music" coming from no apparent source. The sitters recall several variations on the sound, but the most striking was "Taps," played "as on a bell so pure as to bear no vibration—almost as though breathed out without the use of an instrument."[7] Although the hearers were unable to explain it, there were some—among them William McDougall, professor of psychology at Harvard—who expressed reservations, calling the phenomenon normal. The conditions of the musical seances did not preclude the possibility of fraud, and when the possibility exists, the phenomena remain dubious. Other musical effects included the playing of an harmonica,[8] the chiming of a clocklike machine of great size and unlike any clock in the house[9]; the stroking of a gong, like a ship's bell—Walter's "wee watchie"[10]; and the playing of the piano three flights below them.[11]

On the ninth of June, a cabinet was constructed as prescribed by most mediums to aid the concentration of psychic energy. It consisted of a three-part screen six feet tall, covered with a piece of black cloth that hung over the open front down to a level beneath Mina's head.[12] It did not conceal her body sufficiently to allow any bold attempts at fraud.

Clearly the members of the circle were taking the affair seriously, and moving toward a more scientific level of observation. It was Crandon who proposed a trance, urging his wife by describing Crawford's and Lodge's theories of amplification of phenomena when the psychic was entranced. "I will do nothing of the sort," she is reported to have said, arguing that she had such fun watching the proceedings, she didn't want to miss anything.

The doctor rejoined sternly, "Little sister will do exactly as big brother says."

The table moved enthusiastically.

For a few minutes, everyone sat in silence. Then Mina, her eyes tightly shut, began to sway back and forth in her chair, sighing deeply, and touching her cheeks with the backs of her hands. It was done in an altogether uncharacteristic manner, as if she were pantomiming the actions or gestures of someone else. Suddenly, she sat up straight and said, in a terse but audible voice, "I *said* I could put this through!"[13]

From then on, Walter developed as an apparently independent personality, his wit and knack for double entendre soon taking complete control of the seance activities. He was a most un-spiritual spirit, unique in spiritualistic history. Soon much of the English-speaking world was hearing of the ghost who swore and of the Boston society woman who could bring him through.

Who and what constituted the personality of "Walter"? There are conflicting interpretations and accounts, some distorted by optimism and some by spite.

Walter first manifested himself vocally through his sister's lips and gradually mastered the technique of the "direct voice," or speaking without the assistance of any living vocal organs.

What began as a hoarse whisper evolved over the months to a strong male voice. No observers found any clear connection between the voice and the medium's mouth. Richardson developed a "voice cut-out apparatus" that appeared to isolate the voice from Mina's. It consisted of a mouthpiece into which Mina blew along a long tube; the wind from this expiration supported in equilibrium two tiny luminescent spheres.[14] Although most of the friends of the mediumship could see nothing wrong with it, the VCO apparatus became a focus of the critics' suspicions. Unfortunately, it has been lost and is not available now for close scrutiny. The point is that when Mina was occupied with working this machine, holding water in her mouth, or even snoring, the voice of Walter rattled blithely on.

A great body of evidence, some of which will be presented here, seems to indicate that the voice, in some instances at least, was not Mina's. There is evidence supporting the opposite viewpoint, however, and both sides have managed over the years to reach a disturbing stalemate.

In fact, few of the sitters detected much similarity between Mina's voice and Walter's, or, for that matter, between Mina's and any of the voices that appeared during the first year of the mediumship. An early account of these voices affirmed that "these . . . trance talkers had, from the start, voices which were easily distinguishable from one another and from Margery's normal speech."[15] Later sitters, however, did remark on a kind of similarity. Harry Price noted in 1929, for instance, that Walter's voice sounded very like Mina's when she spoke over the telephone. Francis Russell also observed in 1940 that the major difference between the two voices was one of pitch. This similarity might be attributed to the natural likeness of the voices of any brother and sister.

There was also a singular contrast between the voice when it was "independent" and when it was the result of possession; in the latter case, the intruding entity was identified by "gestures, facial mobility, pantomimes, motor control of the entire organism."[16] Hamlin Garland wrote: "I heard a loud merry whistle, like that of a boy signalling to his fellows; and a moment later a curious gutteral voice was heard that might have come from deep in a man's throat. It had nothing feminine in it. . . . The 'Walter' voice heard while Margery's mouth was stopped was that of a vigorous, humorous, rough-and-ready man of twenty-five or thirty, with such intonation as a Canadian youth . . . would use."[17]

Walter's whistle was in itself a striking phenomenon. It was often heard in a spirited accompaniment to his favorite tune, Drdla's "Souvenir," as it was playing on the Victrola. Usually only a few notes, the whistle was clear and well done, even occasionally beautiful. It is perhaps significant that none of Mina's friends ever caught her whistling absent-mindedly. Richardson was able to write in his memoirs that whistling was "a faculty denied entirely to Margery."[18]

All this, of course, is singularly nonscientific and opinionated. We would ask for something conclusive, or at least possessing a higher degree of reliability. At first glance, Richardson's VCO establishes some confidence in the independence of Walter's voice, but the apparatus was criticized severely as a "cover" for fraudulent activity, as it caused the center of attention to go from Mina to the tiny floating spheres.

One informed and reliable opinion is that of Hereward Carrington, that curious and controversial investigator of the unusual. Although an expert magician, Carrington had been convinced when he was only nineteen that psychical research deserved serious attention. He knew that, in spite of all the trickery that saturated contemporary Spiritualism, there was a residue of phenomena that no legerdemain could possibly explain. In 1908, he had accompanied W. W. Baggally and the Honorable Everard Feilding to Naples to investigate the psychic abilities of the physical medium Eusapia Palladino. In all the years of psychical research, there are few cases that continue to hold as much respect today. The Naples report provides evidence for the reality of unexplained physical effects that has never been equaled.[19] Of the Margery case, Carrington wrote in 1930:

"Throwing the voice" to a distant part of the room, in the commonly accepted sense of the term, is quite impossible. . . . Ventriloquism . . . is quite incapable of explaining the "independent voices" heard . . . at Margery's seances. . . . In complete darkness, the customary illusions and methods could not possibly be employed. In their absence, a large percentage of the delusory effect would at once vanish. The medium might produce an exact imitation of a voice, as it would sound some feet away, but at such close range the illusion woud be completely lost and the voice would be located by the listeners at its real point of origin. . . . If the investigator were standing close beside the medium, there is no known ventriloquial effect by means of which the medium could make a sound which would appear to issue from a point in space *behind* the investigator—as happened . . . at the Margery seance of May 19, 1924, at which Mr. Bird and myself were present. . . .[20]

Bird had his hand over Mina's mouth as the voice spoke.

There are many witnessed cases when the Walter voice occurred at some distance from the medium, or in places quite unlikely for her to reach. If this was a fraudulent display and it was Mina's skill alone that accounted for its presence, how did she obtain that skill? How did she manage to put it over on experts as well as fools? And, more important, *why* did she do it?

That she keenly enjoyed the mystification on the faces of her investigators is evidenced by a story Mina liked to tell:

A very famous psychic researcher from Europe . . . came over to study the mediumship. He held many sittings. He was impressed by the independent voice of my deceased brother which always manifests itself in the seance room. He wanted to be sure this was not my voice, so he held his hand over my mouth and nose. But the voice came through quite as plainly.

"Now, Doctor," I said, "isn't that convincing?"

And what do you suppose he said? "How do I know you don't talk through your ears?"

So you see what amazing things people are willing to believe in order to avoid believing the things they don't want to believe.[21]

What did the mysterious voice in the dark have to say? Did it bring comforting and spiritual messages from the Beyond, for the edification and enlightenment of Our Plane?

Scarcely. Walter's heaven was utterly devoid of angels, to say nothing of harps and golden streets.[22] And as for hell, Walter had no time for it at all. Once he reflected before a group of amused clergymen, "Yes, hell is now completely up to date; we burn oil."[23]

Nor was this jovial ghost above using a "damn" or a "hell" in his conversation. Asked a guest once, "Is that the language of the fourth dimension?"

"No," returned Walter. "Perhaps you did not notice that I am talking in the third dimension, a language for *you* to understand."[24]

Walter showed no affection for organized religion. When asked if he "felt nearer to Jesus," he gave a surprised minister the following answer: "I feel his influence more." Then after a moment's reflection, he added, "That was quite intelligent for a minister, wasn't it? Usually they ask if I have afternoon tea with him."[25]

Mina always claimed to be flattered by those who suspected Walter's acerbic wit was an outgrowth of her own imagination. As one of her friends told her, "I'm sure they would not accuse you of knowing so much if they knew how really dumb you are."[26]

"I hope things are not quite that bad," Mina replied.

Whoever he was, the personality that called itself Walter was an individual possessed of an original wit and a penetrating sarcasm that distinguished him in both worlds. In the years to come, the origins and true nature of Walter became even more enshrouded in mystery—a mystery that has never been lifted.

V

The First Harvard Investigation

IT WAS INEVITABLE that Mina Crandon's mediumship would attract scientific interest, and even more certain that the investigation would stem from Harvard. Holding the prestigious position of head of the department of psychology there was William McDougall, whose vitalistic philosophy admitted psychical research into his worldview without difficulty. McDougall had just completed a two-year presidency of the Society for Psychical Research in England and was exciting interest in that science at American universities. He was willing to approve theses for work in psychic science, and he encouraged his students in what he considered the most difficult and character-building of all studies.

Working under him were Gardner Murphy, who was performing encouraging experiments with telepathy under a grant from the British Society,[1] and Harry Helson, a doctoral candidate. They could not have been more eager to discover a genuine physical phenomenon that could be called "supernormal."

McDougall and Helson began investigating the mediumship on July 1, only a few weeks after its inception. The investigation was necessarily informal and limited because of the restrictions Crandon placed on onlookers.

The first phenomenon they witnessed was an exercise in automatic writing with glossolalia, or writing in tongues unknown to the medium. At the beginning of the seance, Mina arose from her seat after passing into trance, and, now "controlled" by Walter, shook hands formally with McDougall. Sinking limply back into her chair, she began to make marks on paper with a pencil that had been placed in her hand. A message appeared: "We create our world for ourselves; we make our own heaven and hell."[2]

Several more automatic scripts were obtained, many in foreign tongues that Mina allegedly did not know. Walter complained of having too much information to relay from his "gang" over there. The sitters were amused by the "picture of spirits jostling one another out of line to communicate."[3]

An Italian sentence was written that baffled scholars; eventually it was explained by Crandon's bootblack as an unprintable slang expression.[4] At a later seance, Walter relayed a disputed verse from Dante.

As the summer wore on, communications in many languages began to come through. On July 24, Aleck Cross had cause to recall his years in China when General Kein Kuen's ghost appeared at Lime Street. Communications in good French, bad German, and ideographic Chinese, in Swedish, Dutch, Greek, and English followed. Though pleasing to the inner circle, these communications entirely failed to convince the Harvard sitters of supernormality.

But Walter was most eager to prove himself, and from July to November this blithe spirit continued to tip the table in spite of all efforts to stop it. On one occasion, investigators crawled about under the table in an effort to locate the cause of these levitations. They failed.

As the scientists refused time after time to make a positive verdict on the phenomena, Walter's rasping whisper became even stronger and his satiric jibes grew more pointed. "Set a crook to catch a crook," he commented.[5]

One of the most startling physical phenomena was "the dismantling of the cabinet" while McDougall was inside, controlling Mina's movements. When the lights went on after the seance, the nine screws that fastened the arms together were found neatly piled in the corner.[6] This was attributed to the joint efforts of Walter and the Richardson boys. At the conclusion of one particularly violent evening, when the cabinet was in complete disarray, Walter was heard to whisper, "Richardson & Stinson, Wreckers."

After much that was ambiguous, the experimenters determined to conduct the definitive observation on the third of November. They examined the house, from the cellar to the fourth floor. The servants* were locked out of the house and the doors were sealed with wax on which McDougall impressed his thumbprint. Each room, every closet and hallway was inspected carefully. The clocks were inspected for trick devices. There were no observable trapdoors or false walls to admit an unknown accomplice.[7]

Under these conditions a seance was held in the fourth floor room which had become, by now, a "psychic laboratory." There was no dearth of phenomena: the table tipped and slid along the floor; a whistle coming from one of the lower floors rendered Walter's favorite tune, "Souvenir"; with water in her mouth and her hands held by McDougall and Helson, Mina succeeded in producing a few words in Walter's voice; again from the lower part of the house, the sitters heard "Taps" played as though on chimes; at the close of the seance, the clocks in the house were discovered to have stopped in the middle of the sitting. The seals on the doors were intact.[8]

In spite of their precautions, the investigators remained doubtful of the truth of what they had witnessed. "They were able to outline a working hypothesis of confederacy which would account for much if not all of what they had seen."[9] They could not, however, discover the identity of the alleged confederate.

*Although the records are not as complete as they shoud be, we know that at the time the Crandons had a maid named Lydia. Later, they hired a Japanese valet, Thomas Nokouchi.

Dissatisfied, the Harvard group met at Lime Street a few days later for an unrecorded sitting. During this session, the observers watched a piano stool jerking in time to a tune playing on the Victrola. The stool then moved out about eight feet from its original location.

At the end of the sitting, Harry Helson walked about the room, his eyes cast downward, searching for a clue. He stooped and picked up a piece of string that lay on the boards near the rug.

Later the Crandons received a diplomatically worded letter from McDougall, informing the doctor of evidence of cheating. He advised Crandon to break it to Mina as gently as possible, or to send her to his office, where he would tell her. Mina decided to visit the long-faced Scotsman in person.

The interview took place on the afternoon of November 15. McDougall used every tactic—"bully-ragging, threats, cajolery, kindness, persuasion or argument"[10]—to get Mina to confess that the whole affair was a joke. When the blonde medium withstood all attacks, McDougall outlined for her the evidence he and his colleagues had gathered.

Taking from his drawer the piece of string that Helson had discovered, he laid it on the desk before him. Watching for signs of weakening, the psychologist noted no reaction beyond an expression of mild bewilderment. Did he mean that all they had against her was a raveling from the rug?

McDougall explained that he deduced that the stool was pulled by the string to simulate a telekinetic effect. The string led down an old hot-air register in the wall, he conjectured, and was pulled by an unknown accomplice.

But Mina's sense of humor, always difficult to control, suddenly became too much for her. She began to laugh at the distinguished dean of psychology. The stool was pulled eight feet by an eight-inch piece of string leading down a hot-air register that was blocked off years ago?[11]

A few minutes later, Mina Crandon left the office of Professor

William McDougall, F.R.S., M.Sc., M.B., giggling uncontrollably.[12]

The first Harvard investigation was at an end.

The same afternoon found Dr. and Mrs. Crandon on a windy platform at the Back Bay railway station awaiting the arrival of a man who would change their lives. He bore the unlikely name of J. Malcolm Bird.

VI

The Psychic Adventures of Mr. Bird

THE MAN WHO STEPPED down from the train was tall and slim, and people recall that he was good-looking, earnest and personable. He parted his hair on the side, and a mass of wavy brown hair often fell down over his forehead. His eyes, above a long thin nose, were perceptive and cool. He affected bibliophilism, wearing old suits and wire-rimmed spectacles for photographs.

But the most memorable feature about James Malcolm Bird was his sense of humor. Ever ready to laugh at the wit of another, he possessed, in his cool and quiet way, a dry and occasionally slapstick ability to define a situation, an atmosphere, or a personality with the most amusing choice of words. He was a better raconteur than writer, but enough spritely wit filters down to us that we can appreciate his ad lib talents.

For all that, Bird had an impressive background in science and journalism. After graduating in 1913, he remained at Columbia University for three more years. During that time he was an assistant in mathematics at Cooper Union and an instructor in the same subject for extension courses offered at Columbia.[1]

Bird was in all respects quite normal and devoid of the morbid interests that often attract men to psychic research.[2] He was married* and at the age of thirty had become associate editor of

*Although Mrs. Bird (née Katherine Alice Montgomery, of Louisville, Ky.) appears in some photographs of seance phenomena, she played very little part in the life of Mina Crandon.

one of America's best popular science journals, *Scientific American.* Intelligent, witty, capable, Malcolm Bird soon made his presence felt at the offices of O. D. Munn, publisher and editor-in-chief. Bird impressed Munn with his knowledge of Einsteinian thought, and was secretary to the committee that ruled on the journal's 1920–1921 essay contest on Einstein's theories of relativity and gravitation.

Bird was one of the people who was drawn into the growing interest in psychical research. Fascinated by little-understood facts of nature and of the human personality, it was inevitable that he would become interested in this murky and mysterious scientific endeavor. Lacking background in the literature and in actual experience, Bird pored over the two major European works of the time. He read and later reviewed for the magazine Charles Richet's *Thirty Years of Psychical Research* and Schrenck-Notzing's *The Phenomena of Materialisation.* Public reaction to his open-minded report on telepathy encouraged him to approach Munn about further articles on psychic science.

The result was the famous *Scientific American* contest announced in the pages of the magazine, beginning in December of 1922:

ANNOUNCING
$5000 FOR PSYCHIC PHENOMENA

As a contribution toward psychic research, the SCIENTIFIC AMERICAN pledges the sum of $5000 to be awarded for conclusive psychic manifestations.

On the basis of existing data we are unable to reach a definite conclusion as to the validity of psychic claims. In the effort to clearing the confusion, and to present our readers with firsthand and authenticated information regarding this most baffling of all studies, we are making this offer.

The SCIENTIFIC AMERICAN will pay $2500 to the first person who produces a psychic photograph under its test conditions and to the full satisfaction of the eminent men who will act as judges.

The SCIENTIFIC AMERICAN will pay $2500 to the first person who produces a visible psychic manifestation of other character, under these conditions and to the full satisfaction of these judges. Purely mental phenomena like telepathy, or purely audible ones like rappings, will not be eligible for this award. The contest does not revolve about the psychological or religious aspects of the phenomena, but has to do only with genuineness and objective reality.[3]

Bird was named committee secretary more for his enthusiasm than for his knowledge of the field, and he began finding the proper people to serve as members. After much thought he chose Professor William McDougall, Hereward Carrington, Dr. Daniel Frost Comstock, Dr. Walter Franklin Prince, and Harry Houdini.

William McDougall agreed to participate in order to give publicity to psychical research and save the science any embarrassment from an incompetent committee. Carrington, a professional investigator of mediumistic claims, had been a member of the Society for Psychical Research since he was nineteen years old. Comstock, until 1906 a member of the physics department at the Massachusetts Institute of Technology, had since devoted his time and energy to inventions. Perhaps his best-known endeavor was the Technicolor company, incorporated in 1922, which would be of signal importance in the development of the film industry.[4] Walter Franklin Prince was research officer of the American Society for Psychical Research. An ordained minister and a skilled psychologist, he involved himself with psychic phenomena as a natural complement to his other interests. He was noted for his painstaking studies of the Doris case of multiple personality and of several significant cases of mediumistic fraud.

Harry Houdini, still famous in our day, was noted in the twenties for his colorful exposures of spiritualistic frauds. The most emotional member of the committee, Houdini was also destined to be the most controversial. His qualifications included expertise in legerdemain and a professed desire to prove to himself that his deceased mother—"an angel in human form"—survived and could communicate. To date, the great magician had been unable to satisfy himself about this latter question, and was working on *A Magician Among the Spirits,* a poorly written account of his adventures with fraudulent mediums during the previous thirty years.

All the committee had to do was wait; in America at that time there were hundreds of people whose claims were worthy of consideration, and certainly many times that number who made their living by simulating psychic phenomena.

Nonetheless, the number of applicants was disappointing.

Bird began publishing articles much too long for what they had to say, hoping to stir up interest. Although careful readers knew that Bird would not have a vote in the contest, his position as "Secretary to the Committee" as well as the authoritative tone of his articles moved some of the more nervous *Scientific American* people to insert frequent boldface announcements all through 1923 explaining Bird's position.[5] For it soon became quite obvious that Bird was an extremely open-minded man.

For instance, Bird admitted in print that he accepted the reality of telepathy, and he advanced that phenomenon as an explanation for the correct content of mediumistic utterances.[6] To the man on the street this was, perhaps, not such a startling suggestion; but to the scientific community to whom Bird was addressing himself it was a remarkable admission indeed. It was easy to suppose that Bird spoke not only for the committee but for science itself. And to this thought much resentment and opposition appeared.

Dissent was also beginning to appear within the committee. Following a preliminary meeting, Houdini and Carrington ar-

gued far into the night about some technical problem touching
upon the investigation. Houdini frequently called Carrington a
"shut-eye"—a magician who knows fraudulent mediumistic practices but who pretends in public that the phenomena are genuine.
Both Houdini and Prince were disturbed by many of Carrington's
actions throughout his career—such as his claim to a Ph.D. that
he had in fact purchased for $150 from Oskaloosa State College,
a sham college that made a living out of such business deals; and
his road tour with a stage magician, during which he seemed to
give the impression that he was sponsoring the magician's feats
as genuine psychic occurrences. Carrington was one of those
curious individuals drawn to psychical research who are as capable of the most crass sensationalism as of the highest level of
cautious observation and reporting. An eruption of ill feeling was
inevitable, and Bird was already beginning to realize it.[7]

But for now, time was still hanging heavily on their hands and
the separate interests of the committee members kept them apart
until notice should reach them of a worthwhile project. A few
letters reached the offices of the *Scientific American,* many dealing
with spontaneous premonitions and other mental phenomena
that did not conform to the contest restrictions; but one that did
excite considerable interest came from the world's leading
Spiritualist—Sir Arthur Conan Doyle.

The great novelist offered his assistance in the quest; he feared
that these comparative newcomers to the field had blundered in
offering money for a demonstration of spiritual power. Wishing
to convince them that the highest mediumships could be observed without pecuniary bait, Sir Arthur placed his extensive
acquaintance with the greatest of Europeans psychics at the disposal of the *Scientific American.*

Malcolm Bird, assigned to communicate with Doyle, embarked
upon this first of many psychic adventures on February 10, 1923.[8]
For him it was more than an assignment.

A little over a week later, he was shaking hands with one of the most remarkable men of his time. The Good Giant, as the French called him, was over six feet in height and heavily muscled, a physical giant made greater by the nobility that animated his personality. His life had been devoted to the search for truth and to the sanctity of the underdog. His literature had been devoted to the depiction of the spiritual traditions of medievalism and to the struggle for life in a fateful and mysterious modern world.

It was no surprise that the creator of Sherlock Holmes had become fascinated by the last great mystery left to man. With bulldog tenacity and English common sense, Sir Arthur had studied Spiritualism for thirty years before declaring his belief in 1918. He was fortified in his faith when his son, Kingsley Doyle, was killed shortly afterward in the World War; soon Doyle was able to establish contact with the spirit of his son—a full materialization, speaking with his son's earthly voice. Absolute conviction in the reality of these visitations colored the rest of his life. Nothing he had ever done, he once said, nor anything he would ever do could compare in importance with the spreading of the revelation of Spiritualism.

Malcolm Bird, shaking hands and looking into that beaming, walrus-moustached face, was charmed. The feeling was mutual. Sir Arthur was more than pleased to find a man of science who was already on the road to conviction. He was gratified to learn that many of Bird's reflections coincided with his own. Doyle later wrote, "They cannot continue to think I am a credulous fool so long as my observations are corroborated by such a man as Bird."[9]

The Good Giant was eager to get started, and Malcolm Bird shared his enthusiasm. On the twenty-third of February, the lanky American was introduced into his first spiritualist circle in London.

The first medium was John Sloane, a physical and mental psychic who performed in darkness.[10] After a short period of hymn singing, Sloane, a stooped, Scottish laborer-turned-oracle, went into trance and began to speak in several different voices—all untouched by the brogue that marked his normal speech.[11] During the messages of one control voice phosphorescent lights flashed and blinked about the room. Bird was impressed by the voices, but the lights, occurring in complete absence of control, failed to convince him. The in-group consented to place Bird in the seat just to the medium's right. The lights continued to glow eerily at different places in the room even while Sloane's right hand at least was under observation by Bird. Now the American *was* impressed.

Then a voice in the dark said that Bird had taken a walk across the Brooklyn Bridge with a couple of friends at about seven-thirty on a recent Saturday evening. Bird was amazed; he had not walked on the bridge in many years, but he *had* taken a stroll with some friends on the afternoon in question, somewhat earlier than the voice insisted.[12] Perhaps it was a lucky shot in a bevy of misses, but Bird was too keen upon the chase to overlook any possible clue.

This report, published with some trepidation, bore a statement from the editors, as would other articles to come from Bird's enthusiastic typewriter: ". . . it becomes more necessary than ever to distinguish between these serious scientific sittings as reported by the *Scientific American* Committee and Mr. Bird's informal examination of European mediumship."[13]

On the twelfth of March, Sir Arthur took Bird around to see Evan Powell, a man then thought to have been one of the greatest living mediums. Notwithstanding the comparative laxity of control, Bird characterized this as "the best seance that I had in England."[14]

He had already so far compromised his neutral status by writing, after a sitting that month, the following comparatively guarded words: "After attending this and other seances, the occurrence of genuine psychic phenomena of a physical character impresses itself upon me as less improbable than I should have judged it to be in the absence of experience."[15]

Following a brief stopover on the Continent, where Bird observed the elaborate apparatus sitting in disuse at Grunewald's Psychic Laboratory in Berlin,[16] Bird boarded the ocean liner *Olympic* in the now warm company of Sir Arthur Conan Doyle. They were to arrive at New York early in April 1923, the American to participate in the *Scientific American* investigations, the Britisher to continue the lecture tours that later were chronicled in his touching and personal memoir, *Our Second American Adventure*.[17]

Conan Doyle left New York confident in the discernment and fair play that he had come to appreciate in Malcolm Bird. He was, in the words of Sir Arthur, "rapidly acquiring so much actual psychic experience that if he should criticize our movement he is a critic whom we will be obliged to listen to with respect."[18]

When Bird's forays into the occult had been compiled and published as a book, *My Psychic Adventures*, it was reviewed by Walter Franklin Prince. Kindly and justifiably patriarchal in his criticisms, the famous psychical researcher pointed out the merits of enthusiasm and youth and the defects of observation and inference that characterized the writing of Malcolm Bird.

He also added words that were possibly prophetic of a time not too far distant, when the *Scientific American* committee would dissolve because of Mina Crandon. The words were written in a comment upon a too-kind interpretation of slate-writing results with an elderly lady who had charmed Bird's watchfulness, and with whom Dr. Prince had also sat with less favorable impressions. "Mr. Bird," wrote Prince, "if he wishes to achieve the authority in psychical research which I invoke for him, must hereafter avoid falling in love with the medium."[19]

VII

The SCIENTIFIC AMERICAN *Investigation*

WHEN THE *OLYMPIC* DOCKED in New York harbor, no mediums had yet been found suitable for investigation. Then, on the twenty-first of May, Bird met an aspiring eastern medium, George Valiantine.[1] His primary gambit was the production of the direct voice, although he was known to indulge in other physical phenomena and even some occasionally puzzling subjective trance messages.[2]

The Valiantine seances were held in the dark with Bird and several of his associates present. Before the sitting, the medium's chair had been wired so that it carried impulses to a recording device outside the seance room. If the medium left his seat at any time during the sitting, the investigator stationed in the hall would know it.

In the dark, the sitters were touched on their cheeks; their hair was tugged, and their sleeves were pulled. So, Bird reflected, were their legs. For every time a "spirit hand" touched one of the sitters, the recording device registered the fact that Valiantine had gotten out of his chair, for as few as five seconds to as many as fifteen seconds at a time.[3]

When Valiantine was in trance, a faint voice, coming from somewhere near the medium, said what sounded like "Wa-wa-wa." Bird supplied the first name that came to his head. "Yes!" the voice said. Bird engaged in some little conversation with his fictitious friend, the ghost cheerfully replying to every clue supplied it.[4]

Valiantine failed to win the prize.

Equally amusing was the series of four sittings with the Reverend Josie K. Stewart, a frowsy little lady who somehow managed to obtain writing and drawings upon cards held in her hand. Bird soon realized that the Reverend Stewart was substituting cards in the deck for previously prepared ones. At a seance on October 16, Bird informed her that there was no point in continuing the investigation. In tears, the Reverend Stewart agreed.[5]

The last days of October and the first week of November found Bird in the seance room with Mrs. Elizabeth A. Tomson, a medium who had been denounced as a fraud by the National Spiritualist Association. Bird's conclusions seem to bear out the NSA report.[6]

Four days in December were spent with the illiterate Italian medium Nino Pecoraro, whose "control" was none other than Eusapia Palladino herself. That controversial sensitive had recently died, making Nino's claims interesting to psychical investigators everywhere. Tied to a chair with sixty feet of rope, Nino was still able to fill the darkness of the seance room with spirit raps and jingling tamborines. Houdini, wired by O. D. Munn, broke off his tour and, as he doubtless would have described it, "came to the rescue" of the *Scientific American.* When he heard that such a great length of rope had been used in place of the customary hand control, Houdini explained that any escape artist can wriggle free of sixty feet of rope: when tying a medium, the longer the rope, the greater the possibilities of slack. Houdini tied Nino carefully with short pieces of cord and Eusapia Palladino failed to manifest herself.[7]

Malcolm Bird's next task was to write to a Boston doctor, whose name had been proposed by Conan Doyle.

At the Back Bay railway station, on the afternoon of the fifteenth of November, 1923, they met. What they said is lost to us, but fortunately Bird recorded his reaction. Mina Crandon was, he thought, a cheerful, vivacious, and very well balanced woman. She seemed younger than her years and strikingly attractive. Nearly as compelling was Crandon's saturnine urbanity, which struck profound chords in the mind of Malcolm Bird. Their acquaintance would ripen over the years into mutual respect.

During his four days at Lime Street, Bird came to know the dour surgeon and his lively wife. Mina was still laughing about the episode in McDougall's office and the "piece of string."

Bird observed Mina's reaction to the first serious allegation of fraud. She was, he tells us, neither consistently amused nor totally crushed by it. There was no "righteous wrath," which Bird felt "would have been incomparably easier for her to maintain fictitiously than the very impressive multiplicity of reaction which I observed."[8]

Mina was frivolous, but Bird detected confusion and even a touch of pain beneath her humor. Still he was impressed by her spritely intelligence. She was, he writes, "an extremely keen person."

If she wanted to indulge in a bit of sport at the expense of her investigators, [Bird continues] I know no one with the mental resources to do it better, or the ability to get more fun out of its doing. My dominant impression of her, as I brought it away with me after my four days in her house on this first visit, was one of mental alertness; and she has a sense of humor quite as wicked as my own. My visit at this time was made into one continuous circus by the fashion in which that confederacy theory was batted about the house, under her leadership. We agreed that Lydia [the Crandons' maid] would not be a satisfactory confederate; that at the critical moment she would appear in the door of the seance room, with an expression of shocked horror on her face, and the words in her mouth: "Oh, Mrs. Crandon, I forgot to wind up the 'Souvenir' whistle." We agreed that Aleck Cross would not do; that he would trip over his own black threads and betray himself by his clumsiness in other amusing fashions. We would tip-toe about the house, looking for the accomplice under ashtrays and in teacups. If we cracked one joke about strings we cracked a hundred. Mina would gravely point out this, that or the other feature of the architecture or the furnishings, and gravely explain its role in her tricks. And so on *ad lib.*[9]

Malcolm Bird rejected the idea that Mina might be diverting his critical faculties by occupying his mind with her own personality. Her vivacious nature charmed and reassured the man who would stake his intellectual career upon her truthfulness. Of course, another interpretation of Bird's thoughts is possible. It has been suggested, indeed, that opportunism may have been a primary consideration in his cultivation of the Crandons: for, in the darkness of the seance room, Bird could see very clearly the path to fame. The man who could verify an incidence of psychic phenomena would earn a place in history; presumably Bird would enjoy occupying that place. If opportunism contributed to Bird's favorable decision, so did Mina Crandon. One must search with uncommon diligence to find another instance in all the history of psychical research so remarkable as the spectacle of the investigator and the medium "tip-toeing about the house, looking for an accomplice under ashtrays and in teacups."[10] Scarcely less remarkable is Bird's frank confession of these lighthearted shenanigans in a volume that purports to be an analysis of phenomenal psychic occurrences.

Mina's energetic flirtations are well documented; other men than Bird were known to be the objects of the blonde medium's enthusiasm. Whatever the motivation, by the time James Malcolm Bird said good-bye on the nineteenth of November, he had invited the charming medium to enter the *Scientific American* contest.

The reply was warm. Crandon invited all the committee members to stop at Lime Street during their stay in Boston. Even McDougall, who had apologized for the "piece of string" interview, was to consider himself a guest of the Crandons. During the entire investigation, however, the Crandon household was under threat of constant surveillance by one or more of the committee:

there was no seance at which some member or agent of the committee was not present; Bird actually stayed in the house while he stopped in Boston, as did Carrington and a number of others involved in the work. Of course, McDougall lived in Boston, and Prince "preferred to stop at a hotel."[11]

McDougall, Prince and some spectators who were not associated with the committee met for a sitting, prepared to be alert to deception. The seance room on the top floor of the Crandon home was carefully sealed against light leakage; no accomplice could enter through a window on the street or through the only door without admitting a flood of light. To offset the possibility of legerdemain in the dark, Prince and McDougall attempted to exercise complete control over the movements of the medium's body. She would go into her trance with Prince on one side and McDougall on the other, each holding one of her hands and touching one of her feet. Sometimes the men placed their heads on her shoulders to prevent her from bending over without detection.

For these sittings, Mina wore only the dressing gown, slippers, and silk stockings that would become her standard costume. The overtones of sexuality are of little import in the reports of Prince and McDougall (although McDougall was aware of its presence), for these men were practiced investigators in the field; it figured more prominently in the reports of other researchers.

At any rate, both men were unimpressed by the sitting. They saw very little that could be called supernormal, and that minimum was performed under less than satisfactory conditions. Spectators at these sittings included many others, aside from the official committee, and controlling all of these people was impossible.

As the sittings continued, some curious events became standard. One involved an ordinary chemical balance from Comstock's laboratory; it was set on the table before the medium with the suggestion that Walter play with it. Before long Walter was apparently able to manipulate the pans of the scale in red light before Bird's wondering eyes.

Another phenomenon focused on an invention of Bird's and Carrington's.[12] It was "an electric bell, so wired that depression of a telegraph key would close the circuit and cause it to ring."[13] If the bell rang while everybody had a grip on Mina, the conclusion was that someone else—Walter no doubt—had depressed the key. Some inexplicable things did happen to the bell-box; no satisfactory explanation has been offered.

The investigators also witnessed the way in which Walter manifested his presence through the independent voice, even when spectators were close to Mina's head, or hands were clapped over her mouth.[14]

On an evening in June, Bird stationed himself inside the materialization cabinet. Crandon usually insisted on holding Mina's right hand and foot, in spite of the admissions that he occasionally freed her hand, explaining that he knew she wouldn't do anything naughty with it. Bird decided that he would preside over this control; he placed himself inside the cabinet and held the doctor's and Mina's hands and feet with his right hand, leaving his left hand free "for exploring purposes"—as Houdini later cheerfully quoted him. Suddenly the entire right wing of the cabinet was violently torn off.

The wing affected [writes Bird] was the one on my side, rather than on Margery's, so that I was between her and the seat of action; the cabinet was dragged violently about the room for a considerable period, carrying her and me with it; and when the wing was finally got loose, this was effected by forcing nine screws out of their holes in the heavy wood of the cabinet, damaging these holes so that they could not be used again. This was the greatest display of sheer force which we ever got in Margery's seance room.[15]

But most remarkable of all was the first appearance of ectoplasm toward the end of 1924. This material has never been fully

verified by qualified observers, although its occurrence was proclaimed with great enthusiasm by French and German psychical
researchers at the time. Nearly all Spiritualists accept it as the
material from which spirits draw their energy when manifesting;
if the "power" is strong enough, it allows the ghost to "material-
ize" all or part of his earthly body. Ectoplasm (or "teleplasm")
exudes from the bodily orifices of the medium and takes on
external shape. Should white light happen to strike it, the
material withdraws into the body of the medium, often with disastrous results to the health of the psychic. At Lime Street the
ectoplasm was composed of a dark organic material that issued
from Mina's ears, mouth, nose, navel and vagina. Usually it assumed the form of crude hands, wretchedly misshapen, but recognizable because of five clawlike projections from the main
mass.

The investigation was proceeding in a very properly plodding,
methodical way when something happened to force the committee's hand. The enthusiastic Bird, impelled perhaps by mixed
motives, wrote an article for the *Scientific American.*

In an attempt to preserve the anonymity of the distinguished
Boston surgeon, Bird had pondered over a suitable *nom du seance*
for some time before he finally typed out the title for his article:
The "Margery" Mediumship.

The name caught on immediately. Many people came to know
Mina very well without ever knowing her real name.

The newspapers sensed a story in Bird's remarks about the
lovely blonde sensitive. Then came the headlines.

MARGERY, THE BOSTON MEDIUM, PASSES ALL PSYCHIC TESTS

Scientists Find No Trickery in a Score of Seances

Versatile Spook Puzzles Investigators
By Variety of His Demonstrations

Other papers enlarged upon the comparatively reserved *New York Times:* "BOSTON MEDIUM BAFFLES EXPERTS," "BAFFLES SCIENTISTS WITH REVELATIONS, PSYCHIC POWER OF MARGERY ESTABLISHED," "EXPERTS VAINLY SEEK TRICKERY IN SPIRITUALIST DEMONSTRATION. HOUDINI THE MAGICIAN STUMPED."[16]

This last headline caused an historic confrontation between the most versatile medium in America and the most famous magician in the world.

VIII

"Margery" and the Magician

THE HEADLINE THAT reported Houdini "stumped" came as a surprise to him. He had not even been consulted about the investigation; his first knowledge of the committee's work came when he happened to leaf through a copy of the *Scientific American* and saw Bird's first article. It irritated Houdini by its presumptuous recommendations of the personality as well as the phenomena of "Margery." Here was an amateur investigator coming very close to endorsing the mediumship before the committee had come to a decision. Houdini was not alone in his objections to Bird's easy-chair observations; the committee had unanimously censured the rash and easily misinterpreted action.

By this time, enterprising reporters had taken enough interest in the committee's work to shadow a car carrying investigators to the Crandon house. As a consequence, these headlines appeared in the *New York Times* on August 10, 1924:

"MARGERY" IS IDENTIFIED

Boston Psychic Medium Is the Wife of Dr. Le Roi G. Crandon

The cat was out of the bag now, and the public visualized the *Scientific American* on the verge of handing over the prize.

So did Houdini, and he needed to stop it.

From the time of his beloved mother's death in 1913, Houdini had sought to investigate the claims of Spiritualism; since he began that quest, his name had become the curse of fraudulent mediums and the bane of honest ones.

A supreme egotist, he was subject to fits of temper and childish impulses; he was sentimental, dramatic, generous, and courageous; he believed in himself—or in the legend of himself that would become reality even to him. He espoused the magician's theory of psychical research: if he could duplicate by "natural means" the phenomena witnessed in the seance room, then those phenomena were fraudulent. To this theory Houdini brought all the childish enthusiasm and religious zeal of a man both delighted by a puzzle and awestruck by the desperate search to recover a lost love.

For all that, his contribution to psychical research was minimal; to the specialist, Houdini was merely pointing out what was already quite clear: vigilance against trickery must be constant. His own exposures of mediumistic fraud, the reports of which continued to keep his name in the papers, were primarily of the countless "small fish" that plagued every American city with their lucrative hoaxes. Applying his own experiences to the classic cases of psychical research, he concluded that all psychic phenomena grew out of systematic errors on the part of witnesses.

Houdini was able to give a fair demonstration of the truth of this thesis in the case of Spanish medium Joaquin Maria Argamasilla, whose claim to "X-ray eyes" had been endorsed by the Nobel Prize–winning French psychical researcher, Charles Richet. Argamasilla's apparent ability to see through the cover of a closed watch was explained by Houdini's detection of the nimble dexterity that allowed the Spaniard to open the watch so quickly that no one but the trained magician could perceive it.

Such comparatively simple answers were to no avail when

Houdini crossed paths with Mina Crandon in the summer of 1924. Canceling part of his stage tour, Houdini rushed to O. D. Munn and promised to rescue the *Scientific American* from an irreparable folly. His alarm was to some extent justified when he learned that Malcolm Bird was already publicly proclaiming that Margery's phenomena were "fifty per cent genuine at least."

At his first sitting, in July 1924, Houdini controlled Margery's left hand and foot. The bell-box was placed between the magician's feet, as he requested.

Houdini had worn a tight rubber bandage around his calf all day, thus making his lower leg extremely sensitive to touch. After the sitting the magician claimed that he had detected the medium's leg inching toward the bell-box to depress the lid with her toes.[1] He published illustrations explaining the trick, but the drawings, when compared to photographs taken at the conclusion of the seance, are highly inaccurate. Bird later pointed out that the lid of the bell-box was higher than the drawings indicate. Bird argued that the alleged attempt would have required rapid and obvious maneuvering along Houdini's leg and under the chair on which he was sitting.

The magician also claimed that Margery ducked her head under the table to tilt it.[2] And he offered a very sound explanation of another instance of alleged telekinesis.[3] Here, the fact of Margery's head being so placed as to allow her to commit fraud, and the fact of Margery having the clear and logical opportunity to commit another trick, established a much more impressive demonstration that the medium committed fraud in Houdini's sittings.

The committee did not agree with Houdini and urged him to have patience. They suggested that Houdini introduce a control apparatus that was satisfactory to him. So Houdini and his assistant set to work on the production of a "fraudproof" cabinet. It was a heavy wooden box in which the medium would be placed with her head and hands protruding from three openings. It was a hot and stuffy little cell, but Mina agreed to sit in it.

On the twenty-fifth of August, a room was taken at the Charlesgate Hotel for the purpose of a seance. Margery was placed inside the cabinet and the bell-box was set on a table in front of her. In the dark, with the medium shut up inside the box, with a hole for her head and two for her hands—both of which were controlled—the bell-box rang.

The magician claimed that all Mina had to do was shrug her shoulders to burst the brass strips that fastened the front of the cabinet. He was pointedly reminded that the cabinet had supposedly been "fraudproof."

Houdini was unwilling to accept any explanation other than his own and the Crandons' confidence in him evaporated. The doctor was particularly enraged by Houdini's blunt accusations of fraud. Mina was agitated about the uncomfortable restraint of the cabinet and "just plain mad" at Houdini.

Bird had been excluded from the hotel room that evening. Mina phoned to tell him of the fiasco, and the next evening Bird hastened to confront O. D. Munn and Houdini about this intentional oversight. Prince tried to mediate, but Bird was too angry to listen. Houdini finally said outright that he did not trust Bird in the seance room. He did not question the man's observational abilities, only his good faith.

Bird was stunned.

He coldly offered Munn his resignation as secretary to the committee and left the room.

The evening's sitting began almost as soon as Bird left the hotel. This time the cabinet had been stapled, fastened and padlocked by Houdini. He guaranteed that no fraudulent phenomena could be produced under these conditions. Just before extinguishing the lights, Houdini put his hand into the cabinet for a moment's final checkup. In the dark the magician repeatedly told Prince, who was holding Margery's right hand, not to let go for an instant. He repeated the injunction so frequently that Prince became understandably annoyed, and Margery asked him what in the world he was trying to do. The dialogue as recorded by Houdini went:

"Do you really want to know?" I asked.

"Yes," she replied.

"Well, I will tell you. In case you have smuggled anything into the cabinet-box you can not now conceal it as both your hands are secured and as far as they are concerned you are helpless."

"Do you want to search me?" she asked.

"No, never mind, let it go. I am not a physician," I told her.

Soon after, Walter appeared in the circle saying:

"Houdini, you are very clever indeed but it won't work. I suppose it was an accident those things were left in the cabinet?"

"What was left in the cabinet?" I asked.

"Pure accident was it? You were not here but your assistant was."

Walter then stated that a ruler would be found in the cabinet-box under a pillow at the medium's feet and virtually accused me of putting it there to throw suspicion on his sister, winding up with a violent outburst in which he exclaimed:

"Houdini, you God-damned bastard, get the hell out of here and never come back. If you don't, I will!"[4]

As we have had occasion to observe before, Walter was not the most spiritual of spirits. The shock was extraordinary, not only because of the forceful exclamation from the etheric spheres, but also because of Houdini's response. Bird had the account from Mina, who may have exaggerated the magician's reaction. "Houdini buried his face in his hands, groaned, almost wept, and cried out: 'Oh, this is terrible. My dear sainted mother *was* married to my father!' "

Houdini himself later reflected that Walter's outburst "just expressed Mrs. Crandon's feelings toward me."[6] Houdini for once seems to have been guilty of understatement.

Immediately after the seance, the cabinet was searched, and a collapsible ruler was discovered. Houdini accused Margery of having concealed it within her body, to use in depressing the flap in the bell-box. Of course Margery denied it. So Houdini called in Jim Collins, the assistant who had helped to construct the cabinet—as well as most of the "ordinary packing crates" from which the great escape artist released himself. Houdini made the following addition to the record: "I wish it here recorded that I demanded Collins to take a sacred oath on the life of his mother that he did not put the ruler in the cage and knew positively nothing about it. I also pledged my sacred word of honor as a man that the first I knew of the ruler in the cage was when I was so informed by Walter."[7]

With this oath on record, Houdini absolved himself of Walter's accusation. Or so it seemed, from 1924 until 1959, when William Lindsay Gresham published the following story:

Years later, when the Self-Liberator was dead, Jim Collins was asked about the mysterious rule. Collins smiled wryly. "I chucked it in the box meself. The Boss told me to do it. 'E wanted to fix her good."

"But he swore on his mother's grave. . . ."

"Sure—that was *after* 'e told me to do it. By that time 'e 'ad it all figgered out in 'is mind that 'e 'adn't done it. There's one thing you got to remember about Mister 'Oudini in his last years. For 'im the truth was bloody well what 'e wanted it to be." Collins added, with a burst of old loyalty, "But 'e was a good one to work for. Never forgot birthdays an' such. And generous at Christmas."[8]

Milbourne Christopher, Houdini's latest biographer, suggests that the story was invented out of professional malice by a magician who, although unimpressed with Margery's phenomena, also disliked Houdini.[9]

In any case, the confusion was such that the next evening's sitting was most significant for the absence of phenomena. Once again Margery was locked into the box, this time after a careful search. The armholes were boarded up so that only her head protruded. As they sat in the dark, awaiting the coming of Walter, Crandon is reported to have said to Houdini, in an offhand manner, "Some day, Houdini, you'll see the light. If it were to occur this evening, I would gladly give ten thousand dollars to charity."[10]

This free-wheeling bribery may sound audacious. But the entire Margery case, if it is notable for anything, is notable for its audacity. Houdini ignored the bribe, as he had earlier ignored a threat that Mina had unambiguously made at dinner. Again, we cite Houdini's words:

Being afraid that I was going to denounce her from the stage at Keith's Theatre she said to me:

"If you misrepresent me from the stage at Keith's some of my friends will come up and give you a good beating."

"I am not going to misrepresent you," I replied, "they are not coming on the stage and I am not going to get a beating."

"Then it is your wits against mine," she said slowly as she gave me a furtive look.

"Yes, certainly, that is just what it is," I told her.[11]

The seance that evening was a blank. The conditions were probably the severest in which any medium had ever sat. From the Spiritualist's point of view, they were also the least sympathetic conditions in which any spirit had ever manifested. It is no serious argument against Margery's powers that at the moment of her most demanding test she failed to bring her brother's ghost through. A Spiritualist would explain that hostile mental atmospheres disrupt the delicate psychical conditions necessary for communication. After this final sitting, Houdini bragged that he, under these exact conditions, could produce mysterious phenomena by normal means,[12] but he was never able to prove anything against Margery with his stage reproductions of the "Margie-box," as he called the wood cabinet. To all intelligent researchers, Houdini's exposure of Margery's mediumship was highly unsatisfactory and the case itself far from closed.

In the dramatic and often humorous encounter between these two amazing people, Margery emerged substantially unscathed. From now on there was no stopping her.

IX

Mr. Bird Looks Elsewhere

AS MARGERY'S FAME spread across America, the *Scientific American*, reeling from the unfavorable attention of scientifically minded subscribers, urged the committee to hasten toward a conclusion.

In November 1924, the journal published the verdicts of four committee members. An editor, E. E. Free, attempted to state the position of the magazine: the committee, he wrote, was "unable to reach a final and unanimous decision with regard to the mediumship of 'Margery.' "

In much of the newspaper discussion of the Margery case, there has been evident a confusion concerning the relative business of the *Scientific American* and of the Committee so far as this psychic inquiry is concerned. The facts are perfectly simple and have been on record from the beginning. . . . The only duty of the *Scientific American* is to pay the award when we are told to do so. . . . We are not the Committee. It is not our business [and here he undoubtedly speaks for Bird's consideration] to decide for or against the claims of any medium, Margery or another.

The opinion of Prince, chairman of the committee, was given first:

[August 29, 1924] I should have preferred to have more opportunities for attending sittings in the "Margery" case before making any statement. But realizing that the unfortunate publicity which the case has undergone may require that some report of progress shall be given to your readers, I will say what is proper now to be said. So much of an opinion as is possible to give at this time, and by me, is based principally on six sittings at which I was present. In five of my sittings I was one of the immediate controllers, in one so placed that it was impossible in the darkness to form any independent judgment. The fourth and fifth were under a method of control to which the Psychic could and did urge objections based upon purported laws of the phenomena, although consenting to it in advance; the others were expressly approved by her circle. The first three presented physical phenomena, the last three none. Nothing of this nature occurred, the *possible* normal explanation of which was not to me immediately apparent, except one striking detail, but that was unfortunately during the only seance where I was so placed that I could not be a judge of the surrounding circumstances.

I am compelled to render an opinion that thus far the experiments have not scientifically and conclusively proved the exercise of supernormal powers.

(signed)
Walter Franklin Prince

Prince's objection to his placement during the occurrence of that "one striking detail" was later attacked by Bird. He said that Prince was functioning as a member of an investigating committee and was thus expected to depend upon the judgment and veracity of the other members, two of whom were controlling Margery's movements. There is some justice to Bird's complaint. Psychical research at that time did rely heavily on personal opinion and firsthand observations; without such confidence, decisions were rare and, when ventured, were more than a little dubious. So Prince was therefore both safe from the attacks of skeptics as well as secure in his own conscience that he could render no other verdict without wider experience with the medium.

Carrington's opinion was published next. It was the first significant endorsement of the case by an experienced and well-known psychical investigator:

[August 29, 1924] As the result of more than forty sittings with "Margery," I have arrived at the definite conclusion that genuine supernormal (physical) phenomena frequently occur at her seances. Many of the observed manifestations might well have been produced fraudulently— and possibly were so produced. Disregarding these, however, there remain a number of instances when phenomena were produced and observed under practically perfect control. I cite, as an example, the continued ringing of the bell of the "contact apparatus," when both the medium's feet rested across my knees, being held there by my one elbow; both her hands were held firmly in mine, the arms pulled out to their full extent; and her head located by her talking at the time, at my request. The contact apparatus was on the floor; tipping of her chair would not have reached it (as I tested), and her shoes were on her feet, showing that they had not been removed and laid upon the contact board—which, moreover, was rung intermittently, at request. The degree of control I considered perfect, and the manifestation was repeated over and over again.

I am convinced that no snap judgment is of any value in a case such as this; nor will preventing the phenomena demonstrate their non-existence. The present case is peculiarly difficult, for many reasons; but I am convinced that genuine phenomena have occurred here, and that a prolonged series of sittings, undertaken in an impartial spirit, would demonstrate this.

                                        (signed)
                                        Hereward Carrington

There is no serious reason to doubt that Carrington was objective in his verdict, but he had been a guest in the Lime Street spare room many times, second only to Bird. One of Carrington's close friends informed me that Margery was wont to flirt with many of her sitters. One evening before a seance, the sitters— Crandon included—were all present in the parlor when Margery walked up to Carrington and embraced him saying, "Wouldn't you like to kiss me?"

Carrington, whose considerable experience with psychic phenomena had never actually prepared him for so frank an onslaught, was embarrassed, but, he later reminisced, "What was I to do? She was there in my arms. . . ."

Hitherto unpublished correspondence between Grant Code and Prince discloses the fact that Margery often boasted of her influence over Carrington.

Margery liberally tells the story that Carrington made love to her and asked her to sell 10 Lime Street, which is in her name, and elope to Egypt. I personally got some of that story from her. Dr. [Edison] Brown warned me that she was the only authority for it. I asked Bird what he knew and got the story in some detail, including the information that at one time she and Crandon were scarcely on speaking terms, and that Crandon would only be decent to her after a good seance. Bird said that at that time she was making advances to every man in sight and cited some of his own experiences. Houdini reported the same thing and showed me photographic evidence. On the story of Carrington's love affair, Bird said he had no evidence other than Mrs. Crandon's word, but he was pretty sure that Carrington had borrowed a considerable sum from Crandon that he was unable to repay. Bird was much more careful to believe in the mediumship before Carrington than he was before me (April 28, 1926).

I was informed by another old colleague of Carrington's that the famed researcher was fond of reminiscing about this love affair with Margery—complete with such details as time, place, and quality of their sexual encounters. Although I do not repose absolute confidence in this story, at least we may suppose that Carrington was enthralled by Margery. Whatever bearing this sort of thing has upon the factual details of a science at that time so dependent upon the personal equation must be left for the reader to ponder.

After some forty sittings, Comstock concluded that, although the darkness was a strong objection to genuineness, "I have seen enough in the light to awaken a lively interest on my part, and I think the investigation should be continued." He felt that if any single phenomenon occurred repeatedly in good light, he would render a positive verdict. Until then:

My conclusion therefore is that rigid proof has not yet been furnished but that the case at present is interesting and should be investigated further.

(signed)
Daniel F. Comstock

Houdini's one-sentence statement was delightfully characteristic; it was the "snap judgment" mentioned in Carrington's verdict.

[August 28, 1924] Summing up my investigation of the five seances I attended of "Margery," which took place on July 23, 24, and August 25, 26, and 27, 1924, the fact that I deliberately caught her manipulating with her head, shoulders and left foot, particulars of which I have handed to Mr. O. D. Munn with illustrations, and the blank seances and incidents which took place at the last three tests: My decision is, that everything which took place at the seances which I attended was a deliberate and conscious fraud, and that if the lady possesses any psychic power, at no time was the same proven in any of the above dated seances.

(signed)
Houdini

The final word on the committee's investigation came in April 1925. "The famous Margery case," O. D. Munn wrote, "is over so far as the *Scientific American* Psychic Investigation is concerned."

McDougall's supplementary statement, dated February 8, 1925, provided the earliest interpretation of the motivations that may have impelled the Crandons to commit such a grand-scale fraud:

As long ago as November, 1923, when I had enjoyed only a few sittings, I wrote to "Margery's" husband, stating frankly that I was inclined to regard all the phenomena I had observed as produced by normal means, possibly with the admirable design of testing and exposing the gullibility of scientific men who venture to dabble in the field of "Psychic Research." Since that date I have taken part in three series of sittings, eagerly looking for evidence of supernormal phenomena and doing my best to keep my mind open to such evidence. During this period, the inclination described above has grown steadily stronger in the main, in spite of some minor fluctuations, and now has become well-nigh irresistible. . . .

This theory—also mentioned in passing by other writers about the case—would be much more attractive if the mediumship had come to an end in April 1925, when the *Scientific American* publicly announced the termination of the investigation. But Margery and the doctor were very far indeed from retiring on their laurels.

It is significant to observe that the same date which saw Munn's article announcing the termination of the Margery investigation also witnessed the first bow of James Malcolm Bird as a member of the staff of the American Society for Psychical Research. This appointment followed rapidly upon his release from the *Scientific American* editorial board, and it coincides exactly with the resignation of Walter Franklin Prince, formerly the society's research and executive officer as well as associate editor of its journal. Educated as a mathematician, trained as a journalist, fanciful of temper and fierce of conviction, Malcolm Bird represented the society's wish to take a definite argumentative stand on the problems of physical phenomena.

The ASPR was convulsed by internal disruptions stemming from the clash between those who felt that psychical research ought to be ruled by the restrictions imposed on all scientific efforts and those who had made the commitment to the religious implications of paranormal events. Especially interesting to this latter group were the physical phenomena reported by many European researchers but that seemed to be very rare in America. Despite the negative reaction of the *Scientific American* committee, a powerful group within the ASPR became interested in the Margery case. Prince strenuously objected to this involvement with what he felt were dubious phenomena, and, with the appointment of Malcolm Bird as research officer in charge of physical phenomena, he saw no course open but to resign. Bird was not a scientist, but an apologist and a newcomer to a field to which Prince had devoted his life. As Prince later observed in a letter to a friend, "Mr. Bird is a master of the art of insinuation, of the employment of language that squints."

On the sixth of March, a headline in the *New York Times* declared: "DR. PRINCE RESIGNS OVER MARGERY ROW." The article reported that "friends of Dr. Prince charged last night that a clique, headed by Frederick Edwards, President of the Society, had practically forced his resignation by stripping him of all authority to investigate psychic phenomena and limiting his sphere entirely to mental manifestations. Dr. Prince is regarded by the Edwards group, so his friends asserted, as being 'too skeptical.' " Many influential ASPR members had been disappointed in Prince because his extensive knowledge of mediumistic trickery had enabled him to arrive at a fraudulent explanation of every case of physical phenomena he had investigated.

Bird suavely informed newsmen that "the field gradually enlarged until there was more of it than one man could do." Two days later, Houdini heard of Bird's appointment with characteristic panic. He immediately announced to the press that he had resigned from the ASPR. For good measure, he publicly accused Malcolm Bird of "helping" Margery in the *Scientific American* investigation. Before long, McDougall added his own resignation to the growing list of psychical researchers who had become disenchanted with the ASPR.

Bird's first article in the ASPR *Journal* was, believe it or not, a review of his own book, shortly to be published, on *"Margery" the Medium.* The review was favorable.

But trained researchers found the book less than satisfactory. Prince himself, now research officer for the Boston Society for Psychic Research, an organization formed in order to preserve scientific standards in parapsychology, submitted an article to the ASPR *Journal* that showed, with "documentary evidence . . . that Mr. Bird twisted and distorted facts in his possession, including some plainly recorded in the official notes of the sittings."[2]

The *Journal* rejected this article, beginning a policy of suppression of all evidence unfavorable to the Margery case. Moreover, in July of that year, a virulent *ad hominem* attack on McDougall's role in the Margery investigation was contributed by so objective an authority as Dr. Le Roi Goddard Crandon. In short, Bird took the society with him as he dived headlong into the Margery case, making extensive use of his new position of authority to publicize the marvels that occurred in the old house on Lime Street.

And, at the Crandon household, this new ally was welcomed with open arms, perhaps most exuberantly by Walter, whose fondness for the new research officer resulted in his being dubbed "Birdie." Walter had already expressed his feelings in a poem composed on the evening of April 27, 1924:[3]

To J. Malcolm Bird

There was a young man from New York.
As a scientist he was a whale.
The mediums came from near and from far,
For him to put salt on their tail.

And he did it without any doubt;
And he did it with every great glee.
And would you believe it: the son of a gun
Is chasing with salt after me.

X

The Dingwall Investigation

JUST BEFORE THE *Scientific American* investigation, the Crandons had taken a vacation in Europe; while in London, Mina had performed for several members of the Society for Psychical Research in their rooms at Tavistock Square. One of these observers was Eric J. Dingwall, research officer for the society and, since 1921, special director of the department of physical phenomena for the American group. Dingwall's experience with the physical phenomena of Spiritualism and with the literature on the subject was unparalleled. Well grounded in anthropology and abnormal psychology, Dingwall was a careful student and a perceptive observer. At that seance in 1923, he observed a levitation so pronounced that it had to be either fraud or supernormality—there was no possibility of illusion. He wrote: "To say that the Margery mediumship is one of the most important of its kind would be an understatement: it is, I think, *the* most remarkable hitherto recorded."[1]

During the summer of 1924, Dingwall came to Boston to see the further wonders of Lime Street.[2] The Crandons warmly accepted his proposed study.

Dingwall found Margery "a highly intelligent and charming young woman, exceedingly good natured and possessed of a fund of humor and courage which make her an ideal subject for investigation."[3] Crandon impressed him with his dynamic intellectual earnesty and his striking defensiveness.

Early in the investigation the mediumship took a new direction with the large-scale production of ectoplasm. During Dingwall's observations the dubious stuff took several forms. When he first touched an extrusion, he compared it "to feeling of a piece of cold raw beef or possibly a piece of soft, wet rubber."[4] He was allowed to see it more closely by the red light of a lamp held and operated by Crandon, often without consultation with Walter. The light never harmed the teleplasm, nor did it ever flash until the materializations were complete.

What Dingwall saw as he peered down was a long, thin "tongue-like structure" issuing, not in motion but apparently arrested in its development, from a slit in Margery's robe, beneath which she wore no clothing. Shortly after, Dingwall caught a second look at Crandon's invitation. He now saw a "mass of black substance resembling two inches of the end of a mittened hand . . . almost exactly resembling the hand structure photographed [with other mediums]." At the next opportunity, he observed a "long, tongue-like projection, five inches long and seven inches broad, now extended from the main mass, which also had no longer a clear outline, but was broken up irregularly like amputated fingers."[5] All this was seen by silhouette against a large luminous plaque held behind the psychic formation.

This gray-black twisted hand appeared frequently, and several very interesting photographs exist in which it seems to be definitely organic in nature.

Walter had originated the plan of demonstrating the materialization of teleplasm. Following a discussion with Dingwall, Walter promised to try to produce it in full view by the red light. The first attempt failed to produce anything but some vague patches of light just in front of the medium (light which Dingwall suggested could have been phosphorescent powder applied to her bosom before the sitting, and exposed in the dark by throwing the robe open).[6] The second try proved more successful. While Walter laughed and chatted, and Margery snored peacefully,[7]

Crandon's light fell on a hideous limp and flaccid hand, protruding from Mina's exposed vagina and connected to the umbilical opening.

Walter explained that this would verify the popular belief that materializations were a form of supernormal birth. Dingwall, who concurred with this idea in theory, was disappointed that the red flashes occurred "exactly when the observer does *not* want them."[8]

. . . everything depended upon the growth and reabsorption *being carried out in red light.* What was wanted was not the finished or partly finished product, but the making of the production itself. These "hands" are supposed to grow, to expand, to approach perfection. But we want to *see* the actual extrusion and reabsorption.[9]

The hand, briefly illuminated, was immediately cast back into the impenetrable darkness. Dingwall said he wanted to touch it. Walter told him to extend his hand, palm upward. Thereupon the mass dropped into it, lifeless and inert; soon Dingwall felt stirrings of the teleplasm, not as though they originated in the mass itself, but seeming to come from the movements of yet another hand directly over it, molding the amorphous matter with deliberation. Crandon's official record then reads: "The next red flash showed a fairly well formed hand lying on top of Mr. Dingwall's hand, while at the previous sight only the unformed teleplasm was seen."[10]

This series of events placed the psychical researcher under the obligation of supposing that the first step toward the formation of teleplasm into an animated hand was the materialization of another hand to mold it properly. This assumption Dingwall found himself unable to make. He realized that a positive working hypothesis, either pro or con, would be preferable to his original total openness. He started with Hypothesis I, the phenomena are genuine, and sat back to await the evidence.

By the time the hand appeared, on January 18, 1925, Dingwall's shrewd eye had caught several suspicious, or at least ambiguous, occurrences. But to give his hypothesis every chance he continued, whenever feasible, to allow Crandon his customary control of the right side.[11]

The question of proper control gave rise to a witticism from Walter. One evening Dingwall, and Dr. Elwood Worcester were debating the matter of control with Crandon. Walter broke in to say that Dingwall should have one of her legs, Crandon the other, and "Dr. McDougall may have a wing." After a moment's pause, he added, "Dr. Worcester may hold her nose if he feels neglected.[12]

Dingwall suggested that they could improve the control on materializations by clothing Margery in black tights. European investigators had used them on a teleplasmic medium to assure that the ectoplasm was not some material substance that was smuggled out of her body by legerdemain; the experiment was said to have worked, for the stuff frothed out from the medium's breasts, vagina, mouth and fingers, taking on shapes *after* it had passed through the weave of the tights. But Crandon felt certain that they would hinder the materializations; he and Margery stood adamant on this point, refusing to consider any garment but the customary robe and silk stockings.[13] However, Margery was wont to relate with relish the fact that she gave some of her sittings for Dingwall in the nude. With customary embellishment, Margery told one of her investigators of her Dingwall seances. "The first thing he told me," she said, "was to take off my clothes" (Code to Prince, April 28, 1926).

The investigators had hoped to introduce some elements of control that would make the phenomena self-evidently supernormal. The refusal to consider tights as suitable garments for the materialization seances brought the observers close to despair. McDougall summarized their feelings in a letter to the *Boston Evening Transcript,* February 18, 1925:

It is reported in the press that in a recent lecture Mr. Bird . . . approved "Margery's ectoplasm," and said that the "ectoplasm" issues from "openings in the anatomy." The last statement is correct. There is good evidence that "ectoplasm" does issue, or did issue on some and probably on all, occasions from one particular "opening in the anatomy." The more interesting question is—How did it come to be within "the anatomy?"

In the next materialization another hand appeared, this time moving sinuously and occasionally startlingly against the illuminated cardboard plaque. Again, the black mass was silhouetted in the darkness, lying inert until the squirming motion began and, from the central pulp, "one, two, three, four or five fingers of all shapes were made to suddenly grow out from the mass, some quickly, some slowly. Then a short, coarse thumb, and finally one long projection with a hook on it, in all twelve inches long."[14]

During the fifteenth sitting, on January 19, a photograph was taken that shows a teleplasmic mass apparently issuing from Margery's mouth and left ear.[15] Again it was seen not as a process, but as a product, and it therefore did not strengthen the case for genuineness. Photographs of this and similar extrusions from the head clearly show a thin threadlike strand, stretching across Margery's hair and behind her head, from which the ectoplasm seems to depend; this added a false note for all but the most confirmed believers. Even the movement of the substance in front of the luminous plaque was subject to explanation. "It is," wrote Dingwall, "conceivable . . . that a piece of the substance had been made into a sort of bag-like structure which, when connected with [a] tube and bulb, might be inflated with air from the bulb by pressure of the medium's legs."[16] But the question remained —How?

This Dingwall attempted to discover during the remaining seances. Once, he recalled, when he was allowed to hold the materialized substance, "the medium at once began to turn in her chair and the mass was pulled out of my hand. It seemed simply an elastic bag and crumpled up as it was pulled away. I tried to follow it when it fell into the medium's lap, but she resisted strenuously, throwing her left leg on to the table and forcing my hand away from it with her own. Another crucial test had failed completely."[17]

Dingwall conjectured that the "ectoplasm" would appear to grow if, after one piece had been illuminated by the red light, it were replaced under cover of darkness with another, larger, more completely formed piece, which in turn would be replaced for the next red flash.[18] It was evident that the stuff was lifeless. At one point, as the materializing ectoplasm was spotlighted, "Margery actually *"put her left hand down, with Dingwall's [hand] still controlling it, and threw the mass upon the table."*[19] Had it been a living, super-normal materialization, the literature of psychical research told Dingwall that the substance would move deliberately and independently; a fraudulent simulation would be inert and incapable of movement on its own, as this was.

Beside the question why?—the pathological implications of which really stagger the imagination—there remained for Dingwall two questions: "How was the materialization produced?" and "What was the ectoplasm made from?"

The majority of the materializations seemed to exude from "an opening in the anatomy." Dingwall asked a gynecologist if this bizarre hiding place would actually be capable of providing an answer.

"Yes," she replied, "of course it would be quite possible to pack a considerable portion of such substance into the vagina, and this could only be definitely excluded by examination immediately before putting on tights. By muscular contraction (which, however, I should think would be obvious) the substance might be held or partially expelled."[20]

As to the composition of the material, McDougall pointed out that enlargements of the photographs taken on January 19 dis-

played "certain ring markings which strongly resembled the car-
tilaginous rings found in the mammalian trachea. This discovery
led [McDougall] to the theory that the 'hands' had been faked
from some animal lung material, the tissue cut and joined, and
that part of the trachea had been used for the same purpose."[21]
McDougall submitted the photographs to Dr. W. B. Cannon,
professor of physiology at Harvard and to Dr. H. W. Rand, associate professor of zoology. Their opinion concurred with McDougall's that "the ectoplasm undoubtedly was composed of the lung
tissue of some animal."[22]

The only objection to this verdict was offered by Crandon; he
maintained that it is nearly impossible to extract all the blood
from lung tissue and that, if it were done, it would cease to
resemble this substance. Also, under normal conditions, blood
would leave obvious traces on the table and bathrobe, and none
were ever remarked.[23]

Midway through the investigation, Dingwall observed something "suggestive and exceedingly interesting" pertaining to the
Walter voice. During the photographed seances that evening,
immediately after the magnesium flashed into the darkness, Walter's characteristic laugh rang out and, at that instant, Dingwall
saw the left corner of Margery's mouth drop and the right corner
raise suddenly, spastically, "as if pulled by a string." Dingwall no
longer had any doubt that the laugh was produced by Margery's
own mouth.[24]

On January 31, Dingwall was scheduled to give a lecture on the
Margery mediumship at Jordan Hall in Boston.[25] He asked
McDougall, his friend and colleague, to preside as master of
ceremonies before the crowded house. Much to McDougall's
alarm, it appeared that at that point Dingwall was convinced of
the genuineness of the phenomena he had been observing at
Lime Street. In a letter to famous European psychist, Baron von
Schrenck-Notzing, Dingwall had written: "It is the most beautiful
case of teleplastic telekinetics with which I am acquainted. One

can freely touch the teleplasm. The materialized hands are joined by cords to the medium's body; they seize objects and move these. The teleplastic masses are visible and tangible upon the table, in excellent red light. I hold the medium's hands; I see fingers and feel them in good light. The control is irreproachable."[26]

On the evening before the lecture McDougall took some time to point out the possibilities of fraud in these seances that Dingwall had apparently overlooked. Not that Dingwall naïvely imagined all the phenomena to be genuine, but on January 30 he did favor a positive verdict on the case. Thanks to McDougall, on January 31 he delivered an entirely objective and neutral lecture.[27]

Later his close friend and colleague Everard Feilding pointed out that "circumstances led him to box the compass of most opinions and to end with none."[28] Indeed, in a letter to Crandon some months after his visit, Dingwall wrote: "Those who have read [the paper] have all come to different opinions as to the real views of the author."[29] While there is in Dingwall's report much that is both unique and eerily exciting, there is nothing convincingly genuine; and while there is much that is dubious and even damning, there is no direct evidence that fraud actually did occur. Dingwall summarized wryly: "We neither know what teleplasm is nor what it may resemble. For all we know formations (if they exist at all) *may* be just like sponges, white paper, chiffon, lungs, or rubber bulbs."[30] But he asked the reader to admit that such a possibility was unparsimonious at best. We may recall here W. H. Salter's remark that spirits of the dead may, indeed, inhabit such grotesque forms as these, but "if so, we must endure the prospect with fortitude."

Dingwall felt that he had failed in his attempt to establish the genuineness or fraudulence of the Margery mediumship.[31] With the information he had at his disposal and the observations he had made himself, it is difficult to imagine how he could have done differently.

But neutrality can also be called fence-straddling, which is what Crandon pronounced it in his reply to the Dingwall report. With characteristic sting, he described the author's fear of derision and the well-known caution of the Society for Psychical Research about pronouncements of genuineness.

From start to finish Mr. Dingwall has not produced one scintilla of probative evidence that the "Margery" phenomena are not supernormal. He has propounded a multitude of theories of infinite variety as to how these things might have been done normally. I have a better theory still. An accomplice small in stature, clothed and hooded all in black, with felt slippers on, could wheel in a tea-wagon with well oiled rubber wheels. It would contain "a rod" (p. 100), "a piece of apparatus to be held between the teeth" (p. 100), "a half-dozen different objects covered with a substance" (p. 105), "forceps" (p. 106), "a glove-like sheath" (p. 106), "forceps covered with animal substance covered with saliva" (p. 106) (possibly an extra dish of saliva in case the first should dry too soon), "a piece of same cut into disc shape" (p. 106), "several pieces cut like sheeps' tongues" (p. 106), "a round mass of same possibly inflated" (p. 106), "a rudely formed hand of same" (p. 106), "a tube" (p. 107), "a cord of some animal gut" (p. 114), "a bulb" (p. 114), "a bag-like structure" (p. 114), "a nozzle" (p. 122), "a long hair with wax on it" (p. 140).

No matter how good the control of "Margery" and myself, the show would triumphantly proceed, unless a cold in the head should cause the accomplice to sneeze! . . . I am tempted, using the words in a purely Pickwickian sense, to lay down two hypotheses to explain Mr. Dingwall's treatment of the subject as far as hypothetical explanation goes.

Hypothesis I: The author is a nut.

Hypothesis II: The author is a nut.

"The evidence seems to me at one time for and at one time against" one or the other of these hypotheses. . . .[32]

A footnote explained the word "nut" as "an American word meaning an amiable individual whose ratiocination is erratic."

Dingwall has never publicly altered his neutral stand. In a private interview with G. H. Estabrooks some years later, he did "express his suspicion of the whole thing,"[33] and in a recent letter he informed me "for the record" that he had no private information that would shed light on the genuineness or fraudulence of Margery's phenomena.

His deservedly famous report on the Margery mediumship ends with these words: "The mediumship remains one of the most remarkable in the history of psychical research. It may be classed with those of Home, Moses, and Palladino as showing the extreme difficulty of reaching finality in conclusions, notwithstanding the time and attention directed to the investigation of them."[34]

No prediction of any occult seer could have proved more accurate.

XI

The Second Harvard Investigation

DURING THE LATTER part of Eric Dingwall's series S. Foster Damon, of Harvard's English department, invited to a sitting Hudson Hoagland, a talented graduate student. Both men were curious about psychical research and had become sincerely fond of Margery. Shortly afterward, Hoagland proposed an investigation stemming from Harvard. The Crandons welcomed the plan even though the proposed group was composed of amateur researchers.[1]

Hoagland planned to publish his findings as a doctoral thesis should they constitute a "contribution to learning."[2] Accordingly, Hoagland, Foster Damon, Grant H. Code, Robert Hillyer, John Marshall, and eminent men from the Harvard faculty and the Boston area formed the second Harvard committee to investigate the alleged powers of Mina S. Crandon.

Mina was characteristically amused by the development. Later she said to an interviewer, "You want to know what it feels like to be a witch? You know that's what they would have called me in Boston 150 years ago. And they would have hauled me before the General Court and executed me for consorting with the devil. But now they send committees of professors from Harvard to study me. That represents some progress doesn't it?"[3]

The Crandons agreed to hold the seances outside of Lime Street, and the investigators used a small, square room on the third floor of Emerson Hall with the permission—and indeed the keen interest—of the psychology department. The first test sitting was held on May 19, 1925.[4]

Before the seance, Dr. Deborah Fawcett made an external search of Mina in an adjoining room and found nothing suspicious on her body or in her robe or slippers. Mina then put luminous elastic bands on her forehead, ankles and wrists to aid the investigators in seeing her movements during the occurrence of phenomena. Crandon, sitting at Margery's right, was also equipped with similar control devices, as were Code and Fawcett. Hudson Hoagland controlled, both visually and tactually, both of Crandon's hands and Mina's right hand, which was placed in her husband's fingers. By placing his forearm properly, Hoagland was able to control the doctor's knees; and, by watching Crandon's luminous headband, he could observe the movements of the medium's most probable accomplice. John Marshall maintained visual control of all the feet around the table, while one of the others watched the headpieces.[5]

Those who had been at Lime Street had already observed and even touched the sort of teleplasmic formations Dingwall had first seen. Damon had touched a hand that moved and could pick things up. From the Crandon record of May 1, we learn that several sitters had seen the moving hand emerging from somewhere in the medium's body. "The wrist muscles were felt . . . then the firm core in the wrist was felt by all, and also tendons which slipped under the exploring finger like the drumstick of a fowl."[6]

The early months of 1925 had also seen the beginning of what would soon become part of the "standardized seance": the levitation in complete darkness of luminous objects, most particularly a small straw basket and a wooden ring that Walter dubbed his "doughnut."

At the May 19 sitting, the Harvard committee saw the teleplasmic arm against the vague light of the luminous plaque, but Walter did not permit them to hold the plaque close enough to allow careful observation of the supposed terminal.[7] Hoagland was impressed with the eerie materialization that occurred while his control of Crandon's hands and the medium's right hand was perfect. There was no light but the luminous bands on each sitter, and these were carefully watched by all the sitters.

John Marshall asserted that he had sight of the bands throughout the sitting; later he told newsmen, "I saw a luminescent something about four inches (as near as I could judge) from the psychic's legs. At the same time I noticed a definite diminution of what little light there was from the anklets, as if some mass of varying intensity was passing between me and the light." He thought it looked like a "ribbon waving lazily in front of a ventilator."[8]

Professor Harlow Shapley, the noted astronomer, was one of the extracommittee observers present at the Harvard sittings. He confirmed Marshall's testimony: "The medium's luminous anklets were at times lost in the luminous haze that appeared to surround the medium's ankles. The anklets, when clearly distinguished, were near the centre of the luminous phenomenon. . . . No evidence of trickery of any kind was observed, and no suspicious actions on the part of any one in the circle."[9]

Walter was in top form for the Harvard scientists, even under conditions of control that the investigators claimed made fraud "impossible." Professor Edwin G. Boring, one of the sitters, was nothing less than effusive with newsmen three months after the investigation ended. He endorsed the presence of an arm, invisible in the dark, but certainly there. It is not clear that he meant this as a statement of belief in a teleplasmic appendage, but readers of the day assumed that if Boring entertained reservations he would have made them known. Thus, when the story broke in the papers it appeared as though the findings had been favorable to the mediumship. Because of this the committee hastened to make their views perfectly clear.

Most of them had strong reservations about Margery's

phenomena. Throughout the eight sittings, despite the elaborate controls, it seemed to some that the phenomena could be produced if one of the medium's legs or arms were free.

For instance, the Walter voice (which Hoagland located as coming "directly from the medium" and which, "though differing in certain qualities, resembled her own in many respects"[10]) was often projected through a megaphone that did not function when a committee member was controlling the link between Margery and Crandon. "Furthermore, on one occasion, when Mrs. Crandon's headband was unusually bright, we observed its reflection on the megaphone directly in front of Mrs. Crandon's face."[11] There were certain restrictions on the investigation that limited the certainty of any statement that could be made about the phenomena the observers witnessed. "We were not permitted to touch or pull any teleplasmic arm without Walter's permission, nor were we permitted any light, white or red, during the seance. Further, we must not without Walter's consent expect to be able to use new methods, apparatus, or controls."[12]

Mina never permitted an internal search, although Dr. Fawcett testified that during two of the sittings Margery wore sanitary napkins, ordinarily discounting the likelihood of internal concealment.[13] (Later, Dr. Fawcett suggested that this may have been a ruse on Mina's part, but no mention of this was made in the record or even immediately after the sittings.)[14]

This may be the place to comment on the often-heard suggestion of anatomical concealment. Despite Dingwall's testimony that "a considerable portion" of artificial ectoplasm could be hidden within the vagina, two remarks by Bird should be considered. The first concerned the frequently observed coldness of the teleplasm.

I may remark that this coldness, continuing long after the production of the hand, affords one of the major obstacles to the belief that this is a normal artificial object, brought forth from the obvious locus of anatomical concealment. One adverse critic was sufficiently impressed . . . to postulate a refrigerating device of some sort, which remained concealed in the region whence the hand came![15]

In the present case, when the suggestion was made that there was another teleplasmic hand, a clawlike member that groped about the table, touching the sitters' hands and being felt in return, the sitters suggested (much later) that this moving hand was a mechanical apparatus withdrawn from "the region of her lap." Says Bird, "The hypothesis of anatomical concealment, taking it at its intrinsic value alone, is stretched far past the breaking point. Mr. Hoagland and his collaborators from the Department of English are under an obvious misunderstanding as to the size, shape, and other dominant characteristics of the anatomical storehouse which it is customary to mention under the gentle euphemism 'within the medium's body.' "[16]

This last would also require Margery to slip her controls, but the committee was confident that the controls made fraud "impossible." "At most of our Harvard sittings we had an apparatus arranged to pass a slight electrical current through the entire circle of sitters, the circuit being closed by the joining of hands and instantly registering with the observer in the hall in anyone broke the circle."[17] As a matter of fact, Margery could easily have dodged the device simply by placing Crandon's hand anywhere on her naked flesh.

But there were always enough people present at the sittings to watch the luminous bands carefully. If Margery had worked a foot or an arm loose, who was more to blame, Margery or the committee? It was a well-known fact that any entranced medium would take the easy way out if that way were left open for her. It was the investigators' duty to make the controls such that only genuine phenomena would appear. Moreover, at no time during the series does the record indicate that the luminous anklets were removed or lost sight of, and yet telekinetic phenomena occurred regularly.

It was not until the seance of June 29, at Hoagland's house, that the flaw in the visual control became apparent.

The committee, in an effort to learn more about the nature of the teleplasm, had decided to use modeling clay as a surface upon which Walter would press his terminal. Walter guessed that the print that would be left would look like coarse skin.[18] When the lights went out, the Walter terminal proceeded to touch the sitters, who recorded their impressions into a dictaphone. Code said that he was touched by something that felt like "the fleshy part of hand, rather rough." Dr. Hilbert F. Day, a surgeon, said that he was touched by "something feeling like the palm of a hand." Another said that it "resembled a heel pressing on his head," while Hoagland "described the sensation as that of pressure from a soft leatherlike object." Walter thought that a good description.[19]

When Code was placed in Crandon's position at Margery's right, a newly designed bell-box rang and an illuminated spool was toyed with despite the change in the controls. Walter tried, but failed, to tie a knot in a rope, which had been dabbed with luminous paint. Crandon prepared a pail of hot paraffin so Walter could produce wax gloves such as those obtained in Europe, but "Walter would have none of it."[20] Then Walter made the prints in the Plasticine.

Later during the seance Walter's terminal was holding up the luminous "doughnut." A "visitor from the Middle West" (probably Dr. Wolcott of Minnesota) blew vigorously at it and dislodged it from the grip of the tentacle. Walter, angered, instantly regained hold of the "doughnut" and challenged the stranger to try to do it again. This Wolcott was not able to do. While this interchange was going on, Hoagland seized the opportunity to see a silhouette of the terminal against the bright illuminated plaque. Later he wrote, "What I saw holding the doughnut appeared to be a human right foot, the toes clamped over the periphery of the disc, creasing it in a way verified by examining the doughnut after the sitting. Further, by shifting my position, I clearly saw the ankle and leg silhouetted to a point above the knee."[21]

Hoagland did not read this observation into the record, keeping it to himself until he could discuss it with his colleagues after the Crandons had departed. At about this point, Code looked down and saw a complete luminous ring on the floor, where before he had seen only the semicircle of Margery's glowing anklet. It was clear that the anklet had been removed. Code immediately reported this discovery into the dictaphone, and, as quickly, the ring became a semicircle again, apparently by obscuring half the ring with a foot. Walter denied Code's statement, but not before nearly everyone had had a split-second glimpse of the full ring lying on the floor. When the lights were turned on, the anklet was on Margery's foot, but stretched from the instep to the heel instead of around the ankle.[22]

Although Mina said nothing about the curious behavior of the luminous band, she was undoubtedly working her mind overtime in an effort to explain it away. She and the dour surgeon left after she had agreed to leave an imprint of her own foot in clay, for comparison with the Walter print.

It was on this night that her slipper fell into the grass.

Now the investigators faced a delicate problem. On the one hand, they had the reputation of Harvard to consider, and so had to give a verdict on the Margery mediumship. On the other, they had the friendship of both Crandons to consider.

Grant Code, the committeeman closest to Mina, felt most deeply the sense of responsibility to her. At the same time, he was certain that he could duplicate the Margery phenomena himself. An amateur conjuror and contortionist of no mean ability, Code conveyed this idea to his fellows and proceeded, in the dark—and later in the light—to free his leg and produce the same eerie effects they had all seen earlier.[23] All present concluded that most or all of the phenomena they had witnessed during this and the previous six sittings could be explained by the normal action of

Margery's legs. It did not occur to them to wonder at John Marshall's inability to catch on to the repeated trick of slipping the band off under the cover of trance restlessness, nor did they consider that the luminous bands Mina had worn were new ones, much larger than usual. Code had made them himself, judging their size from his own ankles, as he "did not have Margery's handy" at the time. So the Harvard committee believed that all the phenomena observed could be explained; they now set out to formulate controls that would make fraud by this means impossible. They could then look forward either to a complete halt in the phenomena or to a radical change in the effects produced.

They settled on the use of surgeon's plaster, daubed with luminous paint, pasted on the medium's legs. From this control, no medium—not even Margery—could possibly escape.

The next morning, Hoagland's dog trotted in with a mauled object that was identified as one of Margery's seance slippers. The examination of the clay prints on the previous evening had disclosed minute particles of sand from the floor, as well as strands of lint. The prints themselves were recognizable imprints from the coarse skin of the human foot, with the whorls clearly visible. Comparison, however, between these prints and those taken of Mina's feet was impossible, for the impressions were blurred and indistinct.

A minute examination of the slipper was undertaken, with the following damning conclusion: "Traces of lint were found freshly pressed into the plastic surfaces, which in color, texture, length of fibre, and material corresponded exactly with the lint of the medium's slippers. Further, under the microscope, tiny traces of sand, presumably picked up from the floor, and the microscopic skeleton of an insect were found freshly pressed into the plasticine."[24]

It looked as though Margery were about to be trapped.

But that night, June 30, 1925, Mina sauntered confidently into

Emerson Hall and chided all the young men for allowing her to wear anklets so big that they would "fall off." After the application of the surgeon's plaster, Margery went into trance. The voice in the dark came through immediately and gave them all the surprise of their lives. Walter told them he knew all about Code's duplication of the phenomena and described certain particulars of their conversation on the previous evening. Even Hoagland was shaken by this display of "uncanny knowledge." For the first few minutes, it looked very much as if the committee's decision had been premature.[25]

After many caustic gibes by Walter, the phenomena commenced. Code, at Margery's right, assured everyone that the control was sound. With a sinking feeling, Hoagland observed that all of the phenomena previously produced came through unchanged. But then he detected that the teleplasm was quite different. Now "long, tapering fingers" were seen, instead of the stubby processes earlier observed. And the reach of the terminal, measured at earlier seances, was much less than the previous measurements had indicated.[26]

Walter allowed the sitters to touch the hand. It "felt cold, moist, and flabby. The fingers were long, cordlike structures, and articulation was very poor in a hand-shaking process." Hoagland noted "slight but distinct movements of Mrs. Crandon's right arm band correlating with the movements of Walter's hand."[27]

If Hoagland's hypothesis of fraud were correct, then these observations would naturally lead to the inference that, despite apparent control, Margery was able to manipulate some kind of an artificial mechanism.

Plasticine imprints were taken again this evening, leaving no coarse skin markings as previously observed, but showing, instead, the "impress of a small, chainlike structure, presumably used to aid in the mechanical manipulation of the artificial hand."[28]

The actual record of this sitting fails to mention the hypothesis of the artificial hand. In fact, the committee found itself dumbfounded by the June 30 seance; Hoagland admits that he was for a moment nearly forced all the way to a favorable conviction. At the end of the seance, Margery smiled pleasantly as if to say, "Explain *that* if you can!" And then she and her husband left.

Within two days Grant Code—a nervous, disheveled man always clad in mismatched jacket, trousers and sneakers—called a committee meeting. The rest of the committee listened with care to his theory of the motivations and the methods that lay behind the Margery mediumship.

Code said that he had himself released Mina's right hand by slipping the luminous band up onto her forearm. Furthermore, this action was the result of a previous agreement between himself and Margery! After the release, "she then proceeded to remove various objects from the region of her lap with her right hand, the bathrobe being thrown open in the dark, and to manipulate them on the table."[29]

"All my observations of Dr. Crandon," Code continued to explain, "had pointed to his belief in the phenomena and a profound religious faith which he based on them I therefore feared that a sudden exposure on the part of a group of observers in which he had placed so much trust would give him a shock that might be dangerous."[30]

Code had decided to confront Mina herself with everything they knew. The morning after the seance of the twenty-ninth, Code visited Lime Street. Mina was apparently alone when Code arrived, except for a woman who opened the door for him and then retired to the sewing room while Margery and Code went to the adjoining library.

Margery sat down to listen to Code, whose presence at Lime Street was no unusual occurrence, for he had come frequently to the house during the last few months. He had, in fact, grown very dependent upon Mina's more stable personality and had often discussed with her some of his most personal problems. This contact with the Crandons had made Code confident that they were sincere about their belief in the mediumship. Now he had to reconcile that confidence with what appeared to be inescapable evidence of fraud.

He therefore formulated a theory of motivation behind this long and intricate charade. Mina had been influenced by Crandon's deep interest in psychic matters, Code told her, and this influence eventually became a "suggestion" in the clinical sense of the word. Once Margery had allowed herself to fall into a hypnotic state, it was easy for the suggestion to grow and take shape in her mind. Gradually, the personality of Walter developed from this unconscious process.

Code went on to say that the committee had accumulated evidence of trickery of which he believed (or hoped) her to be unaware. There were many reasons, he said, for them to suspect that the phenomena were simulated by normal means, not the least of these being the fact that Code had duplicated the phenomena usually produced with Walter's help. He emphasized that neither she nor Crandon could be considered responsible for these actions, as they were both in an abnormal state of mind.

Mina asked what she should do about it. "Her reaction toward the description of the feat," reported Code, "was incredulity and bewilderment."[31]

Code thought for a moment, and then made a suggestion. He would slip her wristlet up on her arm during the seance that evening, freeing her hand to produce the usual Walter phenomena. Otherwise, he hinted darkly, the effects of the unavoidable exposure on Crandon would be harmful for his mental stability.

Finally, Margery responded. "You frighten me, Code. . . . But I don't know what to do. I'll do something for you I've never done for anyone else. I'll give you my word of honor that I have never done any of these things."[32] Here the major point of controversy appears. Code said that it would be easier to deal directly with the secondary personality, and asked if he could speak to Walter. Then, he alleged, he accompanied Margery to the fourth floor where they sat at the seance table and Mina went slowly into trance. Full daylight flooded the room as Code sat at her left, holding her hand. Then:

Convulsive movements freed her hand, which I permitted to escape. It then took a position as if held by a sitter on the other side, the tips of the fingers lightly clipping the edge of the cabinet. Then Walter's voice came through the lips of the Psychic. It was thrown against the wall of the cabinet and reflected so that the exact position of the sound was very deceptive to the ear.[33]

Code told Walter the uncomfortable position he was in. Walter could only say, "Whew!" And, over and over, "What are we going to do, Code? What are we going to do?"

Code offered his assistance. What did Walter want him to do? Walter thought for a moment and then told him to free Margery's hand, and Code nodded and said he would. "Don't fail me, Code," Walter is supposed to have pleaded. "Don't fail me."

Code convinced his colleagues of the truth of the story and the cogency of the psychiatric diagnosis. "We believe," the final report read, "that a large number of Margery's phenomena have been produced by automatisms aided by a high sensitivity to suggestion and a certain amount of amnesia."[34]

Before long, this story reached the press. In late October the *Boston Herald* picked up the story. Most of the large papers soon joined the *Herald* in following the controversy. Two articles were favorable, with the word "hypnosis" conspicuously absent. In them Professor Shapley made an apparently unambiguous statement about the absence of evidence of fraud, and Marshall testified to the luminous phenomena observed around Margery's feet. Then, on October 23, the following headline appeared in the *New York Times:*

'MARGERY'S' FEATS CALLED TRICKERY

Harvard Scientists Now Say Hypnosis Theory
Was Advanced to Spare the Crandons

SITTERS SIGN A STATEMENT

Her Husband Denies the Charges and Emphasizes
the
Change in Their View

Now that everything was out in garbled form, it became essential to publish a complete report; written by Hudson Hoagland, it appeared in the *Atlantic Monthly* of November 1925. It was met with considerable reserve by the psychical researchers, although it was thought by the general public to be the final word and the definitive study on the Margery mediumship. The article was even entitled, perhaps somewhat ambitiously, "The Climax to a Famous Investigation."

In England, the Honorable Everard Feilding, himself one of the world's most experienced investigators of physical phenomena, was moved to write:

The theory of the real innocence of mediums caught *flagrante delicto* is a favourite one among Spritualists, but while I am not prepared to deny that in certain cases, where no apparatus is used, it may, and probably has, some validity, I think that to apply it to such a case as this, where long, elaborate and skillful preparation is indispensible, argues an unsophistication of intellect, to put it mildly, which I can scarcely believe possible in a Harvard graduate. But apart from this capacity for reasoning, Mr. Code's ideas of the line of conduct demanded by friendship on the one hand, or loyalty to colleagues on the other, seem to be little less than pathologically peculiar. To save "Margery" from an exposure he leads her—it must be assumed under pledge of secrecy—into further fraud, and then immediately, that very night, splits on her.[35]

Furthermore, Feilding went so far as to actually doubt the truth of Code's agreement with Walter. "That Mrs. Crandon would be so innocent," he wrote, "as to fall into a trap laid so openly is, to judge by all one has heard of her extremely alert intelligence, at least as unbelievable as Code's theory of her sweet natural guilelessness if the phenomena are fraudulent."[36]

Although Bird predictably attacked Code's allegations, he was unable to give any explanation at all of the incriminating evidence of the Plasticine print, which he called "the serious side of the Harvard case." He did suggest, however, that so much of the mediumship was impressively verified that one or two anomalous instances should not tip the scales against the bulk of genuine phenomena. "Such anomalies," he said, "we therefore leave open to interpretation at some later date."[37]

Following the publication of the "notes" of Code's seance with Margery, in the 1926 *Proceedings of the Society for Psychical Research,* it became evident that any denial of Code's allegations must be officially notarized. Accordingly, Mina recorded her affidavit, saying that no private seance was given Code. Beside her own testimony, another document was included that added more detail and a new perspective. The woman who let Code in was a witness to the entire interview. Her affidavit was in substantial agreement with that of her employer, although she could not be certain of the date of Code's visit.

We may remark that her testimony, resting as it does upon an uncertainly dated memory nearly two years old, matched against that of a man of nearly certain integrity falls somewhat short of absolute trustworthiness.

But these were not the only lines on which the Harvard report —and, in particular, Code's testimony—was attacked. Bird wrote Code a letter threatening to make public an apparently extravagant letter that Code had sent Mina during the time of his greatest emotional dependence on her. From all accounts, this still-unpublished letter appears to have been nearly hysterical, and Code later told Prince that he regretted having written it.

Rumors were set pointedly toward Code suggesting that Crandon was on the verge of bringing suit against Code for an amorous attack on Mina. This never happened, for the purpose was solely to intimidate and silence the newly married English instructor. Prince, however, took the precaution of asking Mina directly about this rumor of legal action before a witness. She denied such action was intended and stated that "Mr. Code was always a gentleman to me." This statement, witnessed by Prince and his brother, was carefully filed in the event of any such problem.

With admirable humor, Code replied to Prince on April 28, 1926, as follows:

The idea that Dr. Crandon was going to prosecute me is another flourish of which I had not heard, added to the story liberally circulated against me .It has come back to me from the most various sources with a number of details that could only have been contributed by Margery, facts picked up in private conversation with me, for instance, and used to touch up the story and make it more convincing to my friends. The first I heard of it was from Griscom, who spread the story that I had made love to Mrs. Crandon, and lost my job at Harvard in consequence, and was now in hiding in Delaware. I have it in writing from Bird that Margery originated the story, with which Bird artfully threatened me. Mrs. Crandon flatters herself as she did when she tried to vamp Houdini! It is very good of you to take the precaution of protecting me as you did. I fancy the case is not likely to get into court. Dr. Crandon threatens suit on every provocation, but I notice that he never sues. In the meantime, as far as I can make out, with a few exceptions the dear public is convinced that I made violent love to Margery and betrayed my associates in consequence, was detected by Dr. Crandon and President Lowell under pressure from Houdini and the Pope, confessed, and fled to Delaware, wherever that is, somewhere near Dakota, isn't it? Much good may the belief do them. It seems to amuse Margery and I can't see that it hurts me.

Nearly a year later Code learned more of the details of the story. In a letter to Prince dated April 11, 1927, he wrote that a visiting investigator "told me among other things how serious the charge against me was that Dr. Crandon proposed to make at one time. I had it from several sources, including Bird, that I was charged with having made love to Margery, but I didn't know before that I was supposed to have attempted rape! I am therefore even more indebted to you. . . ."

The point is that once again, in the face of nearly conclusive evidence of fraud, the supporters of the Margery mediumship were able to raise sufficient questions to allow everyone to entertain an open mind on the matter as well as a certain amount of confusion. The Harvard investigation was, in the final analysis, the last and most conclusive popular exposure of fraud. It therefore marks a highly significant turning point in the history of the case. Now that the public at large was confident that the Harvard report had put an end to this very disturbing open question, it was left to the psychical researchers to continue playing their harmless games with Margery.

But for those of us who do not feel that psychical research is a study that plays harmless games, the turning point reached at the Harvard investigation must be seen as a situation leading to a crisis in that most important science. From now on, as the mediumship passed from the public eye into the specific scrutiny of psychical researchers, the defense of the phenomena would come to rest more and more upon matters of personality, and the cause of parapsychology would become divided into partisan camps about this increasingly knotted issue. Without the unstinting efforts of a few clear-headed men, psychical research might well have been destroyed as a scientific discipline.

XII

The ASPR Investigation of 1926

IN THE SUMMER that followed the Harvard debacle, J. Malcolm Bird arranged with Crandon for an exclusive study of the telekinetic aspects of the case, to commence in August. But when he arrived at Lime Street, he found Mark Richardson already working on a project, with the purpose of establishing definite proof of the independence of Walter's voice.

The summer of 1925 had seen Walter manage incredible vocal feats in spite of investigative precautions. But that was not the extent of the wonders that occurred that summer: there were records of identification in the dark of personal objects held by the sitters,[1] and even the unprecedented success of clairvoyantly reading a deck of playing cards without a single error![2] During Margery's sojourn in Buffalo that October and November, the energetic home circle had constructed a new and apparently fraudproof cabinet, with glass on all sides and into which Mina was tied with wire bands about the wrists, ankles, and neck.[3] All this had appeared to strengthen the scientific acceptability of the case; but Bird was acutely aware of the evidential inadequacies apparent to those who were not, as he was, committed to a favorable verdict.

To Bird, the entire case depended upon the validity of the telekinetic levitations, while the independent voice and the teleplasmic features seemed to be merely secondary. Walter, however, had taken an interest in Richardson's plan and was bending every effort to produce a materialization of the normally invisible vocal apparatus from which the voice allegedly spoke. Richardson's place in the affections of the Crandons—Walter included—assured that his plans would have priority over those of others. So it was that, when Bird motored up to Boston to begin his "official" seances, Richardson, Crandon and Walter suggested that Bird might pursue his investigation as a joint venture. Bird acquiesced reluctantly, hoping to make the best of the situation.

Several months later he stood before the Board of Trustees of the ASPR, reflecting upon the developments he had observed during those summer sittings: the materialization of Walter's "voice-box," a dense mass formed "like a rubber ball . . . hanging out of the teleplasm . . . to a length of about a foot," depending from a cord from the main mass[4]; and the sitting of August 13, during which he had seen the "dim red light for two seconds [showing] the mass of teleplasm overlaying the entire face. It [was] rather heavy in texture, of a general veil-like effect. The cord [was] visible, at the right, running apparently . . . downward at least as far as the right breast." This formation Walter (with some coaching from Crandon) called his "laryngeal extension" —the hideous gray substance sometimes emanating from the medium's nose, sometimes from the mouth.[5] It was during this seance that Bird made the following mental note: "Once or twice during the evening Walter said 'larnyx.' I had never before noticed any tendency on the part of Walter or Margery to mispronounce this word. But the next day she duplicated this mispronunciation."[6]

Despite these marvels, Bird was disappointed that the Crandon group did not share his enthusiasm for a series of definitive experiments in telekinesis; in his report to the board he finally concluded, after having reviewed some of his most trying moments with Walter: "On every ground, it seemed best to confine my future work with Margery to the scientific aspects; and for the Society either to abandon the task of proving here and now, to the man in the street, whether the mediumship were valid or not, or for it to seek a new agency through which to attempt this proof."[7]

Henry Clay McComas was a very charming man; he was also a respected psychologist at Princeton University, currently enjoying a leave of absence for the first 1926 academic semester. His familiarity with psychical research was not extensive, but his experience was growing with his interest. His desirability for the office vacated by Walter Franklin Prince was quite fortunately equaled by his availability. Accordingly, the Research Committee of the American Society for Psychical Research on Bird's recommendation, invited McComas to join the staff.

McComas, attracted by "more generous pay than any university dreamed of at that time,"[8] met with the committee to discuss the possibility of heading a commission to pronouce upon the validity of the Margery mediumship once and for all. With some trepidation, McComas greeted the committee one afternoon late in 1925, "expecting to find gentlemen with long hair and wild eyes."[9] He was more than a little surprised to find men of intelligence, wit, and humor interested in these occult phenomena; and he was even more pleased to learn that he would be given every freedom in the selection of his co-committeemen. They would use investigative methods as rigorous as science would demand. "All we want," they told him, "is an honest study of the facts."[10]

One of the men, probably William Button, a leading New York lawyer, gave McComas a guarded description of some of the Lime Street phenomena.

Within a few days, the door at 10 Lime Street was opened by Nokouchi, the Crandons' Japanese butler, and Henry McComas met Crandon. Crandon's suave urbanity and evident sincerity disarmed McComas and he found himself scarcely able to retain his critical attitude. Years later McComas recalled that "when Mrs. Crandon was presented she would completely upset all preconceptions of the famous medium. A very attractive blonde with a charming expression and excellent figure, the 'Witch of Lime Street' proved to be a thoroughly feminine lady with the best traits of a mother and housekeeper. Her vivacity, with the doctor's poise and dignity, made them a delightful pair for an enjoyable dinner. Both had a very diverting sense of humor and the conversation would never lag."[11]

It was all, McComas observed, "atmosphere." He was the first to interpret the importance of the pre-seance preparation he experienced. Frequently treated to dinner, warmed with wine and pleasant conversation, the sitters were given a short talk by Crandon in his quiet, well-modulated voice, and shown photographs of teleplasmic manifestations. They might then meet Dr. Mark Richardson—"You could not fail to like him," McComas tells us truthfully—[12] and his wife, members of the "Advanced Circle." Richardson's evident belief was impressive. The presence of Dr. Edison Brown and a man introduced as Judge Hill (few sitters were told it was not a title, but a nickname) further impressed the newcomer—and this persuasion before the beginner had seen even a single "psychic" phenomenon! Once the Princeton psychologist ascended the stairs to the fourth floor and was comfortably seated in the dark at the seance table, he met Walter, "the most intriguing personality of all."[13] Crandon introduced the newcomer as Henry Clay McComas.

"No," said Walter, "I am clay."

Margery, fastened securely within a glass cabinet, with wires about her wrists, ankles and neck, went into trance. Walter then took over and a basket was placed at Mina's feet. The basket had been daubed with luminous paint, and now all the sitters could see it rise slowly off the floor, then fly back within the cabinet. Walter explained that an ectoplasmic terminal had caught it up. Then the glass door of the cabinet was opened and a box of carved wooden letters was placed before Margery. Walter felt around in the box, throwing out letters in the dark. A thud sounded at McComas's feet and Walter whispered, "Here's an M for you, Dr. Mac."[14]

Sure enough, McComas picked up a wooden letter M.

These trifling tricks occupied much of the Margery program ever afterward and became a major part of the "standardized" seance, which represented a kind of mock-reply to the long-time criticism of psychical research, namely, that the phenomena could never be established until repeatability could be attained. In most of these seances, insufficient precautions were taken to provide against the possible entry of an accomplice. It must be admitted, however, that most of them would not require an accomplice; their banality and transparency make it difficult to ponder them seriously.

But one puzzling phenomenon that night did arrest McComas's attention. An unopened pack of cards was brought into the seance room and put on Margery's lap inside the glass cabinet. The sitters heard the pack being opened in the dark and then the sound of cards falling lightly on the table one at a time. As each card was drawn from the pack, Walter told them what card he had tossed out. When the lights were turned on (at Walter's command) the cards on the table proved to be the ones he had predicted. The case seemed to be clinched when one sitter wrote something on a card in the pitch blackness and Walter told him what it was.

McComas later summarized his state of mind at the end of that first meeting:

As you would leave late in the evening after saying goodbye to your new and interesting friends, you would probably find your thoughts taking one of two directions. If you had felt kindly toward the spiritistic interpretation of the things you had read about in psychic records you would probably say to yourself: "This is the best argument for my belief that I have ever found." If, on the other hand, your training and habits of thinking made spiritualism impossible you would say to yourself: "What under the sun are these people up to? Are they planning to make a grand exposé of the spiritualists by presenting the greatest show of all and then explaining it? Maybe they are just having some fun, for the evening was full of amusing incidents,—could that be it?[15]

McComas began to select his committee, conferring with two Johns Hopkins scientists, Professor Knight Dunlap, an "outstanding psychologist . . . with a genius for experimental work which is second to none," and Dr. R. W. Wood, "one of the greatest physicists in America," who agreed to participate.

At the sitting of January 30, Wood controlled Margery's left hand and rested his hand upon her knees, while Dunlap held her right hand and controlled her right foot.

All the sitters were careful to retain control at all times. Dictations as to the state of their hold upon "Psyche" (Crandon's pet name for his wife) were made every few minutes. The tense atmosphere finally impelled Walter to mutter in the darkness, "I never saw such a bunch of stiffs in all my life! Talk about dead people; my God!"

The Margery said petulantly, "I am in awful pain, don't feel good anyhow."

Walter replied, "Nobody gives a damn if you are."[16]

After still more banter, the quiet set in again; but at 10:30 McComas made a sudden observation: "Something cold and moist slapped me on my hand."

"Just a moment after, Dunlap remarked that something cold struck him on the hand. I have both of Psyche's ankles in my lap." Then he went on, "My hand just came in contact with a small ribbed substance which was immediately removed from my hand. I have Psyche's left hand in my right." The notes continue:

Dr. McComas: 10.36 Luminous doughnut is placed on the table, and between myself and the doughnut appears a dark, rod-like structure, which waves up and down. . . .

Dr. McComas: 10.37 Walter's voice: "Hold your horses, I will show you in a minute."

Dr. McComas:	10.38 The rod-like structure is lying right across the doughnut. Dr. McComas requested Walter that it bend to right angle. Psyche twisting and writhing as the rod moves. . . .
Dr. Dunlap:	10.47 The "thing" cold and smooth and soft on my fingers. . . .
Dr. Dunlap:	10.50 The "thing" picked up the doughnut in Wood's hand and moved it around against my head.
Dr. Dunlap:	10.51 Psyche presses my hand against "it" again.
Dr. Wood:	10.53 My hand was on the table holding the luminous doughnut, teleplasmic rod fell in the palm of my hand, feeling like a rigid rod covered with soft leather. It was placed between my thumb and finger, which were holding the doughnut. I squeezed it very hard, which produced no ill effect. The rod then slipped through the doughnut and raised it in the air . . .[17]

The sitting ended at 11:33 P.M. One investigator suggested checking both the cabinet and the medium at once. Mina, hearing this, "coughed, gagged, leaned over" as though vomiting. "Then," observes McComas, "aided by the stenographer she hurried to the bathroom, and we could hear a very good imitation of a passenger crossing the English Channel."[18] McComas verified that it was an imitation by inspecting the floor by the cabinet. He found nothing.

Although both Dunlap and McComas saw Margery the next day "in the pink of health, laughing, and talking in good spirits," Crandon later insisted that his wife had been ill for several days as a result of Wood's "rough handling" of the teleplasmic rod.[19]

After this affair it became next to impossible for McComas to arrange a continuation of the commission's investigation.

Wood's conduct at the seances (particularly his apparent intoxication at several sittings) so disturbed Crandon that he refused to allow him to continue on the committee. Furthermore, Crandon had discovered that in 1925 Dunlap had published an analysis of Spiritualism that included the definite statement that all physical means are frauds, pure and simple.[20] This knowledge—not evident to those involved in psychical research—naturally somewhat upset the doctor, no matter how we may regard his part in this curious pastime. He therefore expressed his disapproval of Dunlap as a biased judge. McComas himself was still in the Crandons' good graces, having displayed "conduct above criticism." But Crandon absolutely refused to consider McComas's colleagues. After a year of wrangling, it was apparent to McComas that the commission had failed. In any case, he had come to the conclusion that the validity of the mediumship could not be decided unless Crandon permitted a much more stringent investigation than Margery had ever undergone.

Friends of the Crandons claimed that the present controls were fraudproof; how could these phenomena occur except through supernormality?

McComas faced this argument with characteristic verve and elan: he "produced" a seance of his own. Moreover, he invited members of the ASPR, who were convinced of the reality of psychic phenomena almost entirely through experience with Margery.

Building his program around an Indian Magician who went under the name Ran Chandra, McComas produced two sittings in the offices of the ASPR. "I have fished in many waters," he reminisced years afterward, "and have shot different sorts of game, but I have never known a thrill to match that of saving your medium from an exposure just in the nick of time."[21] While the sitters controlled the medium, McComas was really the one doing all the tricks.

McComas theorized that the best time to have a sitter testify to what he had seen was immediately following the seance. After one sitting—during which a bell-box was rung, voices were heard during the use of a "voice cut-out" device, psychic lights appeared, and playing cards were identified—he had his sitters sign the following statement: "These phenomena were observed by me and I further state that they were done by no normal means known to me."[22]

Fifteen sitters signed this memorandum, yet all the phenomena were produced fraudulently. The identification of playing cards had been the easiest. The cards were placed on the table, and sitters were asked to draw any card and slide it across to the "entranced" medium. In a moment the card was heard sliding back to the sitter, then a voice identified the card. Each sitter remembered what he had been told and then checked after the lights went on. The identification proved to be completely accurate. What had actually occurred was this: while the sitters were building up "power" by singing a song, McComas secretly reached behind him for his top hat and placed it in the dark on the table before Ran Chandra. From the sitters' points of view, nothing at all could be seen. But from the medium's side of the hat, much could be seen indeed—for the front of the hat had been daubed with luminous paint. When the sitters slid their cards to the "psychic," he merely raised them to the light and read them. Of course, the trick had to be performed early in the seance because the luminosity wore down.

The ringing of the bell-box required only trick wiring and a thin thread held between McComas's teeth to trigger the mechanism. It also rang when raised from the table. Thus a sitter could pick it up and rotate it about his head without the cessation of the ringing.

The most complicated apparatus was a voice cut-out machine similar to the one employed at Lime Street. Like Richardson's, McComas's VCO required the medium to blow through a U-shaped glass tube half-filled with water. In each end of the U-tube a cork floated atop the water; when at rest, they were even. Attached to one end of the glass tube was a stiff rubber tube through which the medium blew. The pressure of expiration caused one cork to go down and the other to rise. While Margery's mouth was occupied with the mouthpiece (so constructed that it kept busy both of her lips and her tongue) and the luminous corks could clearly be seen floating unevenly, Walter's blithe prattling could still be heard. So also was Ran Chandra's control conspicuously loquatious with McComas's own VCO. But then, McComas's was admittedly a trick apparatus: small valves, hidden in the rubber tube, enabled the pressure to stabilize when the medium removed his mouth from the mouthpiece.

The psychic lights at McComas's seance were produced with some luminous paint and a flashlight with an infrared filter. This involved some pre-seance preparation of the room, but not much.

Therefore, after a year had passed without receiving a positive go-ahead from Crandon, after McComas had produced his own seance and had duplicated to his satisfaction the phenomena of Margery's "standardized" seances, he decided to close the matter by writing his report to the Research Committee of the ASPR. Dated April 18, 1927, the report summarized the commission's findings and conclusions. The findings we have already discussed; the conclusion was as follows:[23]

In view of the above findings your Commission submits that the Margery mediumship is a clever and entertaining performance but is unworthy of any serious consideration by your Society.

We submit further that the unwillingness of Dr. Crandon to allow the Commission to proceed with the investigation is a sufficient indication that no investigation by competent investigators employing the methods and checks required in all scientific research is likely to be permitted.

Signed: H. C. McComas
R. W. Wood
Knight Dunlap

Once again, depending on one's point of view, Margery failed to produce convincing manifestations for yet another group of skilled observers, or she had succeeded in barely escaping detection in the elaborate fraud perpetrated by the most audacious tricksters in the annals of modern Spiritualism.

But this failure was in many ways the most significant in the whole course of the Margery mediumship, for henceforth the investigation would occupy the efforts and the fidelity of many of the most influential people in the American Society for Psychical Research, involving that science in the greatest scandal in its history.

XIII

Phenomena and More Phenomena

UP TO NOW, we have been largely concerned with the case against Margery; we must also be aware that many people were convinced of the validity of the phenomena she produced. What was the positive side of her case as these supporters saw it?

From November 29 to December 11, 1926, Dr. LeRoi Goddard Crandon spoke at a Clark University symposium on "The Case For and Against Psychical Belief."[1] Also present in person, or represented by papers, were such authorities as Sir Oliver Lodge, Sir Arthur Conan Doyle, Frederick Bligh Bond, William McDougall, Hans Driesch, Walter Franklin Prince, F. C. S. Schiller, Gardner Murphy, Joseph Jastrow, and Harry Houdini.

Because Crandon spoke on behalf of the Margery mediumship, his long lecture serves admirably as a detailed answer to the question.

Crandon described the recent developments in the control procedures:[2]

The upper and lower margins of the [medium's] undergarment are held to the skin by surgeon's adhesive tape; and blue skin pencil-markings criss-cross the margin in all directions. Stocking-tops are similarly covered. Shoes are fastened on with "figure of eight" surgeon's plaster similarly marked with pencil. The Psychic's wrists and ankles are fastened with No. 2 picture wire (strength, 128 lbs.) fastened by square knots and surgeon's knots and the free ends of these four fastened to eye bolts in the floor of the cabinet and to the outside of side-holes in the glass cabinet and the ends closed with railway express lead seals. The parts of the wire going around wrists and ankles are made immobile by surgeon's tape and the position of the tape made permanent by blue pencil marks. The Psychic's knees are wrapped from 4 inches above the knee to 4 inches below the knee with surgeon's tape, binding the knees fast together, leaving no room between them. The Psychic wears, besides the garments already described, only a searched kimono. Her mouth, ears and short-cut hair are searched, and the neck is fastened tightly, to prevent any movement forwards, by a locked leather collar fastened by a horizontal rope leading to an eye-bolt in the back of the cabinet. She sits in a wooden Windsor chair fastened to the floor of the cabinet. The distance from the wire knots to the eye-bolts is recorded. The general outline of the Psychic's body, including arms, wrists, ankles, knees and head are visible at all times by the insertion of 50 large-headed luminous pins. All the lashing is done by the most skeptical sitter present. Under these conditions, the phenomena to be described occur.

Lime Street observers had signed the following eyewitness reports of physical and mental phenomena:

1. *Breezes.* Sitters felt very cold breezes that came from the cabinet and occasioned a drop in the room temperature from 70 to 42 degrees. The only other reliably recorded instance of this was Harry Price's historic investigation of the medium "Stella C." —a case with which the Crandons would have been abundantly familiar, as Price had recently published his report in the *Journal of the ASPR.*

2. *Raps.* These occurred most notably in the early months of the mediumship, but were still occasionally heard in 1926.

3. *Table-tilting.*

4. *Telkinesis by teleplasmic rods.* Similar phenomena to those recorded by the Harvard group—e.g., the moving about of the luminous "doughnut"; the levitation of the glowing basket; the tipping up and the holding down of the table, sometimes against considerable force.

5. *Telekinesis by energy only, without teleplasmic rods.* The ringing

of the bell-box while an observer held it high in the air, turning it around to demonstrate the absence of threads or similar devices that could cause the flapper to be depressed normally; and the experiments with the chemical balances that were just beginning to come into their own as a part of the standardized seance. One pan would be weighted. After it descended, Walter would somehow emanate enough energy to push the other pan down, so that the two were equal. (Walter once said about the procedure, "You have just seen the action of gravity; now I'll show you the action of levity."[3]) Dr. R. J. Tillyard, Fellow of the Royal Society and colleague of Harry Price at the National Laboratory of Psychical Research in London, called these experiments "about as perfect as human ingenuity can devise."

6. *Trance voice.* In the earliest months of the mediumship, the voice speaking for Walter came from the medium's own lips, as in the most common cases of subjective trance mediumship.

7. *Trance writing.* In some seances writings in many languages —all unknown to Margery—were received.* Automatic writing also occurred before seances, giving Walter opportunities to compose poetry. Two lines were particular favorites of the Crandons:[4]

> There is a plan far greater than the one you know;
> There is a landscape broader than the one you see.

The Crandons had these lines made into a rubber stamp; I have seen an autographed copy of Bird's *"Margery" the Medium,* which Mina gave to Richardson, on the flyleaf of which these lines had been stamped.

8. *Musical sounds of supernormal origin.* These chimelike sounds

---

*It must be added here that Crandon compressed the glossolalia into one incredible evening, when in fact the writings were received many evenings apart. Of course, if the glossolalia were simulated, the intervals between the messages would allow Margery to memorize a line or two of some familiar foreign work. It is evident here, as elsewhere, that Crandon was quite unafraid about prevaricating outright.

were heard at the very beginning of the mediumship and
rarely thereafter. Bird tells us that they ceased on the day of his
arrival.

9. *Perfumes.* A somewhat exotic knack possessed by the best
European mediums was the production of sweet scents and ori-
ental odors. It is difficult to imagine how these could be demon-
strably supernormal and Crandon did not elaborate.

10. *Supernormal lights.* Some of these were small as pinheads,
others "twisting columns of luminosity, 2 feet wide by 7 feet
high."

11. *Materializations invisible to the human eye, some of them intangible.*
Photographs, taken by magnesium flash at Walter's command,
disclosed things unseen and unfelt. One remarkable photograph
of the chemical balance shows a transparent cylindrical object
that was not visible to the sitters in red light nor verifiably present
to the touch.[5]

12. *Materializations felt but not seen.* Crandon mentioned the hundreds of times that Walter had touched sitters or allowed them
to touch his invisible terminal. Crandon described the structures
as "soft, rubbery, cold (40° F.), yet feeling as if they contained a
firm core."[6]

13. *Materializations visible and tangible.* Crandon discussed the
teleplasmic extrusions that began during Dingwall's stay and a
new kind of teleplasm that began later. Walter explained that this
was cortical teleplasm, while the familiar grayish stuff was uterine
teleplasm. Cortical teleplasm was often seen to "develop and
spread over the whole head and face of the psychic and pour
down into her lap; though it remains connected with the ear." In
successive flashes of red light, it was "seen and felt to develop
and grow downwards. A great sheet of it sometimes extended
down five feet as it draped over a kind of proboscis arising from
the face of the psychic. This mass appears lace-like in structure,
but that is only appearance. There are really no holes in it."[7]

14. *The independent voice.* Crandon mentioned the independent

Walter voice heard when Bird, Comstock and Carrington at separate times placed their hands over the medium's mouth and nose, while Margery held water in her mouth, and when she was operating the voice cut-out machine. Richardson, wishing to learn more about Walter's respiratory system, had set before the medium "a blow bottle half full of baryta water (saturated solution of barium hydrate). To the inlet tube is attached a metal pipe held by a wooden clamp towards the Psychic, about 30 inches away from her mouth. Her mouth and the apparatus cannot get nearer together. Now the Psychic blows up the voice machine. Walter talks and there is a passage of bubbles through the baryta water. Not only are these bubbles heard, but luminous floating glass pellets may be seen and heard dancing up and down in the baryta water. . . . After the experiment the baryta water showed precipitation of barium carbonate from carbonic acid gas, as from a normal lung."[8]

15. *Apports and deports.* Frequently mentioned in the literature of psychical research, the practice of the supernormal entrance of some foreign object into a locked room was a rare occurrence at Lime Street. On one occasion a live pigeon was apported into the house, but even Bird was notably reticent about making too much of this. Other apports included antique jewelry and flowers.

16. *Paraffin Gloves.* Elsewhere, I have briefly described the beautiful wax molds, allegedly made by ghostly hands, which Spiritualistic seances had been producing throughout the history of the movement. Particularly striking were the famous "spirit-gloves" obtained by Professor Geley of the Institut Metapsychique with the medium Kluski, which for sheer beauty and detail are among the most uniquely persuasive arguments for the reality of spirit materializations.[9] At Lime Street, their first appearance occurred during the first year of the mediumship, under the most unimpressive circumstances, but in 1925–1926, under increased control, Walter succeeded in producing a great many

gloves, all right hands, none the same as the hands of the Crandons or anyone in the room.

17. *Fingerprints.* It might be supposed that the gamut had about been run by Margery and her spritely brother, but their most recent experiment was unique in the history of psychical research. During the course of the paraffin experiments, Walter hinted that his etheric body was such an exact match to that of his earthly one that it might actually be possible to impress his thumbprint in the wax! During a visit to her dentist, Dr. Frederick Caldwell, Mina asked for suggestions for such an experiment. Caldwell suggested that a plate of dental wax known as Kerr would take a very detailed impression. He softened a small piece of Kerr in boiling water and pressed his thumb into it, producing a finely detailed print. Mina asked if she might keep the sample, and perhaps some extra pieces for the experiment. He gladly gave her these, and a new era in the Margery mediumship was begun.

From the first night, Walter was successful in doing what no ghost in all of Spiritualistic history had ever done—he proved his independent identity by leaving a clear print of his own thumb! According to the testimony of a police expert from a large fingerprint bureau, the print established, as Crandon quickly noted, "the presence in the room of a person not one of us."[10]

In the face of this unprecedented array of spiritistic phenomena—the list of which would increase almost monthly— it is certainly understandable that the guiding individuals behind the ASPR, who had given much of their time and fortune to the hope of someday discovering even one genuine phenomenon, should be perhaps overgenerous toward Margery. Few, if any of them, knew anything about legerdemain. There were, besides, personal commitments to be considered. Many of the officers of the society were close friends of the Crandons, and many were especially fond of Mina. Rumors still circulate about Malcolm Bird's special feeling for her, and we will soon examine published evidence that Margery demonstrated her exuberant emotions more freely than discretion and scientific objectivity would demand. It was almost inevitable that these men, thrown into close and even intimate contact with the still strikingly attractive Mina Crandon, would consider the mediumship a special case and would defend the phenomena as they would defend her, thus perverting a gentlemanly confidence in a lady's honesty into an extraordinary plea for the truth of a fantastic hope.

One of the most dramatic, and in the last analysis most significant, confrontations the Margery mediumship ever faced occurred on July 1, 1926. For the man who entered the door at 10 Lime Street on that evening in July was Dr. Joseph Banks Rhine, the man who must be credited with the founding of modern parapsychology.

While writing reviews and comments for the *Journal of the ASPR*, Rhine had met the ubiquitous J. Malcolm Bird, who somehow managed to persuade him that there was a preponderance of genuine phenomena in Margery's seance. Intrigued by Bird's sincerity, Rhine asked if he and his wife could attend a sitting. With Bird's intercession, this meeting was quickly arranged, and Rhine eagerly anticipated this first encounter with the most sensational mediumship in the twentieth century.

On the evening appointed, the young professor and his wife, Dr. Louisa E. Rhine, were treated to the usual friendly dinner, informal lecture, and sprightly conversation. Several close friends of the Crandon family—among them ASPR trustees Joseph DeWyckoff and his wife and Daniel Day Walton, were the "official" observers. The complex seance room on the top floor was not made available for any examination in white light by the Rhines.

The seance began. Walter's voice came through and phenomena began to occur. The two novices noted that, contrary to the popular impression of Walter, "nothing was referred to him." Crandon operated the lights, described the phenomena about to occur, and served as "stage manager."[11] During a demonstration of the scales-balancing phenomenon, Crandon alone flashed the red light on the balance, with no consultation with Walter.

The Rhines observed that the pans reacted to the pressure of Walter's alleged teleplasmic terminal or of his pure "psychic energy" very much as Crandon predicted they would. After one pan was weighted down by checkers, the other would depress more than the weighted pan. These reactions were seen in stages by successive flashes of Crandon's light. The rest of the operations were completed in the pitch dark.

They also saw something not told us by Crandon. When the Richardson VCO device was used, Margery's neck was not fastened to the rear of the cabinet; the collar and neck ropes were removed. The Rhines conjectured that this allowed Margery to bend over until her hands, tied to the sides of the cabinet, could remove the mouthpiece of the apparatus and plug the hole of the tube in some way.[12] After the seance, the two investigators surreptitiously inspected the device and discovered that the "glass mouthpiece was easily removed from the rubber tubing. . . . She could blow up the manometer and hold her thumb over the end of the tubing. . . . Also we do not know," they continued in their report, "that there is not a place where the tubing can be bent back sharply and so closed effectively."[13] The Rhines' criticism of the voice cut-out apparatus discredited the device for all future scientific consideration.

They also noticed that Walter's whistle was never heard simultaneously with the levitation of the little basket. They had seen that Margery's neck collar was released, and the basket on the table was within reach of her teeth if she leaned forward. If the inventive medium "levitated" the basket that way, she would not be able to use her mouth. If Walter's voice came from Mina's mouth, his vocal manifestations would never be heard simultaneously with the levitation of the basket.[14]

Later Rhine saw, with perfect clarity, the silhouette of Margery's foot against the luminous plaque during a levitation of the megaphone through which Walter often spoke. He saw her foot "kicking the megaphone over within reach of her hand."[15]

After the sitting, Rhine also saw that the rider on the balance did not move when he pushed it laterally. Peering closely in the faint light, he noted that "there was a small set screw which turned easily with the fingernail." As he was inspecting the scales, Crandon approached and told Rhine to leave the apparatus alone before he "put the balance out of order." The doctor's peremptory tone put an end to Rhine's Sherlockian activities.[16] But the accusation rested there, unanswered.

If Rhine could stroll onto the scene and detect evidence of trickery, why was Bird, at this time with some three years' experience on the case, unable to see anything suspicious about the phenomenal scales? Could he, with his scientific training, have been so completely fooled? Or was Bird, research officer of the American Society for Psychical Research, Margery's confederate?

Others had hinted at this possibility, and Houdini had said it. Bird, writing in one of the society's publications, provided an answer that was—as nearly all Bird's answers were—somewhat evasive:

One thing must be abundantly clear from the outset, however. Among the hypotheses which must be admitted as the price of rejecting Margery's phenomena is that of active and sustained confederacy by myself. The same remark will ultimately apply to numerous other sitters, but at this moment I am interested in it only as it involves me. My attitude, implied but none the less clearly present in my mind when I wrote my previous book, was that I knew myself to be innocent of this charge and would not quietly submit to it. This, too, is an idea from which I have completely recovered. I have come to realize that to a very considerable proportion of persons, dishonesty from any source whatever, no matter how high, is easier to believe than are the phenomena of the physical seance. This is a perfectly valid state of mind, an aspect of human psychology from which we cannot escape. . . . If the reader is of this type of mind, and if I succeed in reducing him to the plea that I am the confederate or the fraudulent reporter, I regard myself as having done my full duty by him, and as having carried him as far along the road of ultimate education in the facts as it is possible to carry him.[17]

Time and again, Bird ridiculed a valid accusation as a "state of mind" and turned one question into quite another with the suggestion that he was being unfairly persecuted. His words appealed to the natural American sympathy for the underdog, but they failed to appeal to his most essential audience—the critical readers who desired scientific acceptability in psychical research.

Why might Bird as well as a number of his colleagues have been a party to this remarkable game? One suggestion comes from the Rhines:

It is evidently of very great advantage to a medium, especially if fraudulent, to be personally attractive; it aids in the "fly-catching business. Our report would be incomplete without mention of the fact that this "business" reached the point of actual kissing and embracing at our sitting, in the case of one of the medium's more ardent admirers. Could this man be expected to detect trickery in her?[18]

A glance at the records makes it clear that sexuality was present in Margery's performances. Aside from the scanty clothing the blonde medium habitually wore, there were the suggestive control procedures deemed necessary by the investigators. On at least one occasion, Bird attempted to discover the range of Mina's vision in the darkness by placing his arms around her from behind and laying his head aside hers to approximate her eye level.[19] This sort of intimate contact could lead to compromising emotions, especially in the singular atmosphere of the seance room. George Lawton, in his sociological study of Spiritualism, comments on a sitting in which he participated at a Spiritualist camp. Following mention of darkness, heat, and a state of "mild hysteria," Lawton observes:

Here was a dark room, with three men and twelve women, all emotionally wrought up, seated about the room in a very close physical contact. Most of the persons were apparently living sexually empty lives, so that in addition to the emotional excitement [of] . . . the situation [i.e., the attempt to communicate with the dead] . . . there was an excitement of sexual character more or less disguised.[20]

The following sample from the official records of the Margery sittings suggests underlying feelings in the sitter's consciousness:

August 13, 1925: 10:11. Richardson was instructed to give his two leading fingers to the Psychic. They were carried to her face and used to finger the teleplasmic mass. Walter asked Richardson whether he felt skin, and Richardson said he plainly did—a distinct . . . unmistakable skin effect. . . . Gerke, instructed to come near and make the same experiment [hesitated to state at the time the only simile that occurred to him as giving mental satisfaction. He said he would report to Bird later; but Walter ragged him into reporting before the other sitters to the effect that] the nearest he could come to describing the mass was that it felt like a woman's breast.[21]

To what extent Mina consciously contributed to this atmosphere in order to enlist aid and sympathy for this curious endeavor we may only surmise. There is even evidence in Prince's correspondence that makes it nearly certain that Bird was offered a blank check by Mina in payment of his expenses. Bribery of one kind or another seems to have been so common in this case that it is scarcely worth noting: Carrington, for instance, was rumored to have been indebted for a considerable sum to Crandon's extravagant interest in psychical research. What is interesting to us here, however, is the fact that Bird later told one of Prince's correspondents that he had intended to save the check as evidence that he had been offered a bribe, should the course of events ever make such a step expedient. As he came to know Mina better, he discarded the idea and cashed the check for what he deemed the "customary amount." It need hardly be stated that it is far from "customary" for a medium to pay the expenses of those who are supposed to be investigating her.

Another question concerns Crandon's motives for sustaining this state of affairs. The Rhines offer the following:

[Crandon] gradually found out she was deceiving him, but had already begun to enjoy the notoriety it gave him the groups of admiring society it brought to his home to hear him lecture and to be entertained, the interest and fame aroused in this country and Europe, etc. This was especially appreciated by him in view of decided loss of position and prestige suffered in recent years.[22]

Rhine also mentions Crandon's enjoyment of the semiparanoid role, "hailed in many quarters as a 'martyr to the cause of science,' a 'second Galileo,'" and so on. Of Margery, Rhine wrote, "Her difficulties will be better understood if it be mentioned that both she and Dr. Crandon have been married before, and Dr. Crandon more than once. We refrain from publication of other pertinent and explanatory material for reasons which must be evident to the reader."[23]

Bird could scarcely be expected to keep silent in the face of such a convincing analysis. His reply was directed toward the reader's reason, but slighted the facts: "Infatuation for the Psychic is given as the motive leading all these confederates into the game; how then does she maintain this elaborate organization free from any disruptive outbreak of jealousy on the part of any of its members?"[24]

"Outbreaks of jealousy" did occur in the following years, but at the moment Bird had to worry about the case for the reality of Margery's phenomena. He enlarged frequently upon the inability of critics to open their minds, their unwillingness to alter the "philosophy of a lifetime," their noticeable alacrity in accusing investigators of fraud before they would accept the records of seance-room occurrences as honest. He also wrote about his private hopes for the mediumship as history would see it one day: "Is it not evident that there comes a point in Margery's history when we must stop generalizing about her charms, stop generalizing about the human weakness that makes it so easy for her to develop confederacy among her sitters; and ask whether the thing has not gone to a point where the more probable explanation of this long history of alleged confederacy from respectable sources is to be found in some other direction?"[25]

Rhine and his wife did not share Bird's confidence in the "more probable explanation" of genuineness, but were, in fact, quite disgusted and disappointed. Rhine immediately severed connections with Bird. When the ASPR refused to publish the report of their investigation they left the society and became affiliated with Dr. Walter Franklin Prince at the rival Boston Society for Psychic Research.

After the Rhines' report had been published in the *Journal of Abnormal Social Psychology,* they were treated to the usual barrage from Margery's supporters. Rhine tole me recently that Sir Arthur Conan Doyle, furious at this latest slur on the accomplishments and character of the Crandons, bought space in the Boston newspapers and inserted a black-bordered notice stating simply: "J. B. RHINE IS AN ASS."

And the *Boston American* for February 7, 1927, ran the following headlines: " 'I KISSED A WOMAN, NOT MEN,' MARGERY DEFIES CRITICS." In the article that followed, Margery reportedly said, "That's all poppycock. My husband attends all my seances and I would have to be very rash to go around kissing."

But, while the papers tended to support Margery, few serious researchers failed to see the importance of the Rhines' analysis of the case. Moreover, their disillusioned break with seance-room research was fortunate, for in 1927, under the auspices of William McDougall, then at Duke University, Rhine and his wife began their now-famous research on the all-important supernormal mental phenomena. In 1930, an Institute for Parapsychology was founded at Duke that led the way for other researchers for over thirty years. It was Rhine who coined the now-commonplace term for these phenomenal cognitive occurrences: extrasensory perception—ESP.

It may be said that one evening's experience with Margery may have had the good fortune to so repel J. B. Rhine that his search for more stringently scientific controls in psychical research led him to make a more incredible breakthrough in our knowledge of man's nature than science had hitherto revealed.

XIV

The Breath of Scandal

FREDERICK BLIGH BOND was, to all appearances, a stereotypical closet scholar, a little, beak-nosed Englishman with conservative tastes in clothes, a man not understood by his contemporaries, and a mystery to us. The remarkable thing about this unremarkable man was that he had directed the archeological excavations of the Glastonbury Abbey, from 1908 to 1921, by means of the instructive intervention of the spirits of monks who had lived and worked within those crumbled walls centuries earlier.

Bond's work at Glastonbury had been at once a disturbing revelation to his superiors and an elating coup for the Spiritualists. It had caused much heel-clicking in occult circles all over the world, but psychical researchers greeted the news with characteristic wariness.

Looked down upon by fellow archeologists, distrusted for his heretical religious theories by Spiritualists, and somewhat alienated from other psychical researchers, Bond was also hounded by a vindictive wife who, after her divorce, sent letters to one after the other of his employers, charging Bond with nonexistent atrocities.[1] Then an unnamed patroness invited Bond to give a series of lectures in the United States and the American Society for Psychical Research arranged the tour. Bond's biographer, William Kenawell, writes: "For the first time in many a year he seemed happy. He was surrounded by people who were sympathetic to all of his consuming interests. He was getting paid for talking about his loves to attentive and fascinated audiences in New York, Chicago, Baltimore, and Petersborough, Canada, where he stayed with a cousin and basked in their warm welcome."[2]

On the first day of his stay in Boston, Bond met the Crandons. They and their friends at least pretended to believe that Walter Franklin Prince was the source of all adverse criticisms and the most flagrant disseminator of scandalous rumors. It is not too much to suppose that Prince was one of the first topics of conversation, especially since Bond proceeded directly from Margery's house to the Boston Society for Psychic Research. Margery herself, sweet and friendly as she usually was with Prince, phoned to tell him that Bond was on his way.

Prince was eager to see Bond; it had been Prince's intervention that had secured Bond his invitation to speak at the Clark University Symposium on Psychical Belief. They had engaged in friendly correspondence the previous fall, while Bond was editor of *Psychic Science*, a British Spiritualist quarterly. He had written a column filled with errors stemming from an unwarranted belief in the Crandons. When Prince wrote to correct him on several matters of fact, Bond wrote a humble and gentlemanly reply. A reviewer who could accept criticisms gratefully, Prince concluded, must be an honest man in pursuit of truth.

During that first meeting, Bond asked Prince if any new developments in the case suggested a revision of his previous opinion. Prince replied that, far from revising his early views, he considered that the Harvard and Rhine reports had virtually tacked the last nail in the coffin constructed by the *Scientific American* committee.

They discussed the case for some time; it seemed to Prince that Bond was leaning favorably toward the Crandon camp. They parted cordially that afternoon. When Bond returned a few days later, Prince attempted to dissuade the Englishman from an espousal of what Prince regarded as America's most intricate and prolonged fraud. Either by gesture or by directly pointing them out to Bond, Prince indicated that there was information in his files that would someday supply historians with a possible source for understanding the motivations behind the Margery mediumship. Then, for one reason or another, Prince left the room for about twenty minutes.

Bond went to the file cabinets and opened them. His eyes fell upon a letter from Grant Code, dated April 28, 1926, containing the following paragraph:

Do you think there is anything in my idea that in addition to the perfectly obvious reason for never permitting an anatomical examination (i.e. dangerous precedent that might be awkward if appealed to at the wrong seance), Dr. Crandon does not want any investigator to know the precise nature of the surgical alterations he has made in Margery's most convenient storage warehouse? Second only to Dr. Crandon's description of Margery as a simple, guileless girl, is his oft repeated statement of the normal internal dimensions of that same warehouse. In commenting on her alleged profuse menstrual flow, Margery told me that it was partly occasioned by an operation. Now a slight surgical enlargement of the mouth of the uterus would make it a more convenient receptacle, especially if it is displaced. And on Dr. Fawcett's testimony, Margery's "development" is abnormal.

The following is an excerpt from a letter from Prince to Code, dated April 14, 1927:

Bond did peek into a file of mine, to which no right of access was given him, while I was out of the room . . . evidently went straight to *C*, and the devil led him to one paragraph written by you where you alluded to an operation Margery was said to have had, and to its possible convenient consequences. He went straight to the C's with it, and distorted rumors and charges came back. I was said to have been saying that she had an "illegal" operation, then you were declared to have said it. Margery wrote a letter to someone saying that the city was filled with a story about an illegal operation on her—the fact being that whoever heard of the reference to an *illegal* operation heard of it through the distortion and the prying and the treachery of Bond. . . . The fact that Dr. C. performed an operation on M. was printed in the Boston Herald in 1924. . . .

The first inkling that Bond was up to something came on February 8, 1927, sometime after he had seen the file and talked to the officers of the BSPR. In a letter addressed to Dr. Elwood Worcester, president of the BSPR, Bond indicated his displeasure with the recently published report of the Rhines and further asked if Worcester would "send me in confidence the names of the two medical men whom you mention as being in a position to know the facts."

Here he was referring to the rumor that Crandon had been refused a position at City Hospital in Boston because of a misappropriation of funds. Bond wanted to clear the air of a falsehood that might support Rhine's reconstruction of motivations, which Bond considered scandalous and even libelous. He ended his appeal by saying, "I want you to help me to pull 'psychics' out of this very malodorous cesspool. It must be done, and all men and women of goodwill must unite in doing it."

Finding neither Worcester nor Prince willing to enter into an explanation of these scandals, Bond ventured further. Both men received the following letter, dated February 14:

Dear Dr. Worcester,

I am sorry you are not prepared to co-operate with me in clearing the character of innocent persons from what I find to be entirely baseless slander.

I have therefore to act myself, and to act forcibly so that the evil may go no further.

I have interviewed one of the heads of the Hospital who is a prominent and honoured citizen. He says there is not a shadow of truth in any of the accusations I have heard made against Dr. C. as explanatory of his resignation, and he is so indignant that he is ready to take active steps to bring home to the accusers the knowledge that their game is lost.

A speedy Nemesis now awaits the author of the worst of these accusations and innuendos and nothing can save him. You will discover that you have been grossly deceived.

Margery is about the finest medium God ever gave and her subjective work so marvellous that it will suffice to vindicate her absolutely. This work *shall be preserved* and she shall now be protected from any further mischief.

If you had, as President, stood firm against wrong from the first, you would have preserved the usefulness of your Society. As matters are, it will be so gravely affected by what is now impending that I doubt whether you will succeed in holding it together. The present organization is poisoned through and through and its functions paralysed. The re-constitution must be clean and the stain wiped out. Until then there can be no harmony.

Yours sincerely,
Fredk. Bligh Bond

It seems that the "subjective work so marvellous" was nothing less than a series of automatic spirit communications from the pen of the versatile Margery, purporting to be further revelations of the Glastonbury monks. The tone of the letter indicated that Margery had enlisted more than an apologist; she now had a fanatic on her side.

Following a moderately phrased warning from Worcester, Bond wrote another bizarre note, dated February 22, in which he shed further light upon the nature of the rumors out about the Crandons:

The whole matter in a nutshell is this: You have given me plainly to understand that Dr. Crandon was dismissed from his position at the Hospital for misappropriation of certain moneys in his charge. When I told you that Dr. Prince denied this and informed me that the real reason was not this, but "the systematic seduction of nurses," you said that perhaps both charges were true. I then begged you to see Dr. Prince whom you have often assured me you believe to be a most truthful man. I asked you also to inspect for yourself certain records. . . .

I have now to inform you that the statements made orally by you and by Dr. Prince to myself as reflecting upon Dr. Crandon are wholly false as I now know from personal investigation.

What I now ask, on your honour as a Christian gentleman and clergyman is, that you retract entirely the oral charges and innuendos made by you to me against the Crandons, and that you institute action which will secure the destruction of the records of falsehood in the archives of the Boston Society.

In making this request I am as far in motive from any thought of using physical force as I am free from concern at your hint of interference with my own economic situation through an appeal to Mr. Cram* to restrain me.

I am,

Yours faithfully.

Fredk. Bligh Bond.

A few days later, the main blow was dealt. In a piece entitled "An Open Letter to the Boston Society for Psychic Research," Bligh Bond publicly stated that the BSPR was fostering scandalous attacks against the "honor" of the Crandons. He concluded with an invitation to the BSPR to conduct a "full and impartial inquiry" into this business. Earlier attacks had been made on the BSPR; some Crandon advocates had labeled it the "Society for the Suppression of the Margery Mediumship." Steady maneuvering had led the public to believe that Prince desired the destruction of "the best medium God ever gave." But rarely had the Crandon camp enlisted an advocate so readily shaped to their purposes. Bond was willing to imply that Prince was a petty, treacherous scandalmonger; from this it could be inferred that all attacks associated with him were also tainted. In one masterly stroke, the Margery advocates could insult Prince and invalidate the Harvard and Rhine reports.

Although Bond was at first the unwitting tool of the Crandons, it soon became clear that the defensive Englishman had shouldered the case with fanatical zeal, and now promised to become

---

*Bond was employed by Ralph Cram, an architect; Worcester had mentioned that he might be forced to inform Cram of Bond's unusual behavior.

dangerous. But Prince met the challenge squarely. On the day Bond's "Open Letter" appeared he wrote to Crandon, asking if Bond was acting as his agent and, if so, what it was in particular that he wanted investigated by an "impartial committee." Was it the Margery phenomena or the doctor's personal record? This may have given the Crandon group its first warning that Bond's usefulness could turn back upon them. Prince received the following letter, dated March 5:

Dear Dr. Prince:—
In reply to your letter of March 3, 1927, I beg to state that I have no agent.

The only investigation I know about is the one now going on of the slanderous activities of two "amiable, scientific, and Christian" clergymen in the Boston Society for Psychic Research.
Yours truly,
L. R. G. Crandon, M.D.

Dr. Prince replied on March 7:

Dear Dr. Crandon:
I thank you for the information that you have no agent, and that, therefore, the author of the "open letter" in the Spiritualist paper of Boston is not your authorized agent. But since that gentleman is publicly urging an investigation in your behalf or in behalf of the Margery phenomena, or both, in a manner which implies that he represents your wishes; and since the making of such an investigation is contingent on your concurrence and endorsement, and on your definition of the object and the terms of the investigation, I am obliged to repeat, in substance, the inquiries to which you have returned no answers.

1. Does the demand of Mr. Bond represent your wishes, or, in other words, do you demand that an investigation shall be made?
2. Is the subject matter of the investigation to be (1) the Margery phenomena, or (2) your personal record, or both?
3. Will you define what you would regard "an impartial committee"?
4. Will you agree to abide by the public verdict of such a committee, if its subject is the Margery phenomena? In order to know

whether and how to proceed, I am obliged to ask one more
question.

5. If the other matter is, solely or in part, to be the one investigated,
are you willing that the results shall be made public?

I do not like to appear importunate, but it must be known to you that
a man is making himself very conspicuous as your champion, and is the
first man at this stage to make public hints of a certain character, basing
them upon his own violation of confidence. My experience with the
contingencies involved in many investigations made when I was a legal
officer of the State of Connecticut, informs me that I should know,
anterior to any decision, if you assume responsibility for the demand,
just what the demand is, and the terms and ultimate disposition of any
investigation to be made.

> Sincerely yours,
> Walter Franklin Prince

Any reply would commit the Crandons to an embarrassing
course of action: refusal to permit an investigation would vindicate Prince, while to allow an inquiry might bring to light information Prince had gleaned from "physicians, a nurse who
claimed to have poignant knowledge; from others who had
voluntarily said that they knew these charges to be true, that a
former matrimonial partner had made allegations, that certain
newspaper files were said to contain illuminating material" and
so on (Prince-Hyslop, February 26, 1927). Prince's letter was
never answered. Margery, in a cheerful and friendly chat with
Prince,* intimated that she would just as soon let the whole
matter drop.

Prince and Worcester were abundantly satisfied with this decision. Bond's "Open Letter" had failed to stir up the bother that
both he and Prince had anticipated. The attempt to discredit the
BSPR had fallen flat; Prince was willing to let the matter rest.
Worcester wrote to Mina on March 15:

---

*Their relationship was always most amicable. One of Prince's fondest memories
was of Margery visiting him one afternoon in 1926, making him a gift of home-
made doughnuts and a bottle of bootleg Scotch. The bemused Prince, who was
all his life an avid supporter of temperance, received the gifts politely.

My dear Mrs. Crandon:

I have investigated, as I promised you I would do, the accuracy of the statement made to me some time ago by two reputable physicians that Dr. Crandon's failure of reappointment at the Boston City Hospital was due to some question involving the finances of the hospital.

As a result of my conference with Dr. David T. Scannell, who apparently has full knowledge of the reasons which prevented your husband's reappointment, I am convinced that the information I received was inaccurate. As to what the real reasons were, I would suggest that you yourself talk with Dr. Scannell.

As I said to you in our conversation, the information which I passed along to Mr. Bond was at his request and accepted by him confidentially, as I then supposed for his personal guidance and private use as a distinguished psychic researcher. I very much regret that his communication to you of this information has caused you any embarrassment or anxiety.

Possibly I ought to add that Mr. Bond's inquiry was addressed to me personally, and that my answer was personal and not in any way as a representative of the psychical research society with which I am affiliated.

Elwood Worcester

But the meddlesome Englishman refused to let matters rest: he informed the BSPR that he intended to publish the entire correspondence in the *Journal of the ASPR*. When it was submitted, the board unanimously voted against its inclusion in the journal. The inquiry that might have revealed the undercurrents of the case was thus averted; we are left with mere conjecture and bald records of historical fact.

Bond was now forced to channel his energies into an extensive and financially gratifying lecture tour. At its conclusion, in December 1928, "he was engaged by the A.S.P.R. to write a series of articles on his experiences"[3] with the more distantly controversial problem of Glastonbury Abbey. In 1930 he was rewarded for his energetic championing of Margery by being given the taxing responsibilities of editor of the ASPR's monthly journal, formerly the job of J. Malcolm Bird.

XV

Mr. Bird Thinks Twice

IN FEBRUARY OF 1927, the society elected Hamlin Garland, the well-known novelist, to its Board of Trustees.[1] The artist, whose work was so influential to the development of literary realism in America, was fascinated by the physical phenomena of Spiritualism. One of his relatives had been a medium; her life of hardship resulted in Garland's conviction that mediumship was a "tyranny of the dark" that brought sorrow and privation to those born with the faculty. His usual response to practicing mediums was sympathy.

It was the intention of the board to have Garland settle the Margery case. His meeting with the board disclosed that "two of the directors were bitterly opposed to the Crandons,"[2] but that the rest of them were either neutral or convinced of Margery's phenomena. Garland had at least one qualification for the job: "I am," he assured them, "convinced that Mrs. Crandon is the most interesting psychic in America."[3]

In May 1927, Garland wrote to Crandon, asking to attend one of the Lime Street seances. Crandon replied: "I shall be delighted to have you join our circle. Come to dinner. We should be especially pleased to have you as our guest for the night."

Crandon levied one condition before permitting a "test" seance: that Dr. and Mrs. Richardson be present. When Garland readily acquiesced Richardson sent along a few amiable suggestions prior to Garland's arrival at Lime Street. "It might be desirable," he wrote, "to get some of 'Walter's' fingerprints in a locality at some distance from Lime Street. In such a case, would you mind having present Captain Fife, the fingerprint expert from the United States Navy, who has this entire matter in charge?"[4]

They agreed to meet at Richardson's home in Newton Centre, and the expert was invited. This man, John Fife, was the shadowy figure whose signature endorsed the fingerprint identifications in paper after paper dealing with this feature of the mediumship. We were told that he was "Chief of Police, Charlestown Navy Yard"; that he was a Finger Print Expert was attested by the FPE following his signature. Prince was unable to satisfy his curiosity about Fife. The Boston Police Department had apparently never heard of him. Garland himself admitted: "I knew nothing of Captain Fife beyond his alleged position as an officer connected with the Naval Station in Boston, but I granted that his experience as a detective and fingerprint expert made him essential."[5] Crandon insisted on Fife's presence; he wrote to Garland, "He is essential if you wish to secure such evidence."[6] Fife had examined portions of thumbprints found on a razor used by Walter Stinson during his lifetime and long forgotten in a trunk in the attic. He declared that they were the same as the prints in the Kerr wax.

The first meeting set the mood for later endorsements of the Crandon pastimes. One of Garland's Boston friends had said of the Crandons: "He is a charming host and entertains many distinguished guests. His wife, the medium, is young, vivacious, and pretty."[7] And so he found them. Crandon impressed him intellectually; he reacted to Mina with characteristic sympathy for the "gifted." After a brief discussion with Crandon, Garland was told that the seance would soon commence. "A few moments later," wrote Garland, "our hostess, the widely celebrated Margery, came in—a lovely young woman charmingly gowned. She was much younger than I had expected her to be. She was indeed," he added with enthusiasm, "hardly more than a girl."[8] She was thirty-nine.

"She showed no signs," he went on, "of the many gruelling tests to which she had been subjected for nearly four years. She was not only smilingly at ease but humorous in her replies; and yet, beneath her gay mood, I caught now and then a hint of serious purpose."[9]

During the seance, in addition to the promised thumbprint, Garland was vouchsafed a lengthy interview with Walter while Margery was struggling with the voice cut-out apparatus. The heart of the artist went out to the voice in the dark. This was how he wrote of Walter:

> While he could not be *seen*, he was to my other senses as much a personality as the "Katie King" of Sir William Crookes.* He presented himself as a youth, humorous, powerful, impudent, and testy. He ordered us about like children. He assumed the tone of a master, as though by the mere act of dying he had become possessed of all the wisdom of Lodge and Edison, and yet he busied himself with tricks to astonish us like a boy of twelve![10]

Although Garland's account is lengthy and enthusiastic, one passage captures the tone of his "investigation" as well as the curious nature of the man—at once critical and naïve. During standard "perception in the dark" tests, with Walter identifying objects placed in a basket at the psychic's feet, Garland "dropped into the basket a minute object which no toe could possibly lift or define."

> A rustling of the basket followed [he continues], and for a few seconds "Walter" was silent as if *feeling* of the object. At last he said in a puzzled way, "It's a coin about the size of a Canadian five-cent piece." Then after

*Garland here refers to the only significant physical phenomenon never produced in the Lime Street seance room: a full-form breathing materialized phantom. It had been Crookes's peculiar good fortune to have lived in those early days of Spiritualism when such things were common. See Crookes's *Researches in the Phenomena of Spiritualism*, London, 1926.

another pause he added, "It has a hole in it—something like a Chinese coin."

"Bravo, 'Walter'!" I called out. "You've almost got it. If you'll tell me what that hole in the middle of the coin means, you'll win a grand victory."

After another pause, he said: "It seems to have a couple of slits. I can't make it out."

I then said to the other sitters: "The coin is a token such as the railway company in Washington uses. The rough place which 'Walter' feels is the letter 'W' cut out of the coin."

In an injured tone "Walter" asked, "How could you expect me to know that? I never was in Washington."[11]

The reader, acquainted by now with the athletic propensities of Mina Crandon, is invited to speculate on the possibility of a basket at one moment being on the floor in the pitch dark beside her feet and at the next moment being on her lap within reach of her fingers. The possibility of Crandon contributing to the success of this phenomenon is also not to be overlooked.

Despite these obvious considerations, Hamlin Garland's brief experience convinced him of the reality of the Margery mediumship. Beyond this, his sitting accomplished nothing. The society was still in a state of unrest and intellectual turmoil, and the public was ceasing to care very much who was right—if anyone was!

All this while, the overworked typewriter of Bird turned out a series of alternately pompous, amusing, intelligent and folksy articles on psychical research. By 1929, Bird would lecture before more than two hundred audiences all across the country and in Europe on topics ranging from "Fraudulent Mediums I Have Met" to "My Psychical Investigations."[12] He traveled to the Sorbonne to represent Margery's case to the International Congress of Psychical Research and went to Austria to sit with Rudi Schneider, a youth who was producing an extraordinary variety of puzzling telekinetic phenomena. Bird concluded that the

Schneider effects were the result of trickery—that the darkened seance room had been invaded by an accomplice.

Bird's skepticism about Europe's greatest case of physical mediumship made his favorable estimate of Margery's performances even more impressive. His fidelity to Mina was further evidenced as he continued to devote his spare time to the slowly progressing second volume of the *Proceedings.* The Margery mediumship could hardly have found a more energetic champion.

Then came the seance of July 15, 1927.

A new apparatus, called "Butler's Little Theater," was in use. It was a sturdy box with an open front; inside the Crandons had placed a pendulum and some scales for Walter to play with and a device called the "sisyphus," which was a ball-bearing that Walter rolled up an inclined plane with his ethereal powers. During the seances, the open face of the toy theater was encased with glass, providing some assurance that no one was manipulating the objects fraudulently.

The following account of this crucial seance is an excerpt from Bird's original report, very much as he typed it that same evening:

Butler's Little Theater was in use; first with the pendulum, then with the scales; the sisyphus was to have been used but was not reached. The Theater was set on the table, which was slightly quartered, at Margery's left and in front of her; there was ample space for her to enter the cabinet at the east, and the table was not moved over (into its more usual position) after she entered.

Almost immediately on extinction of the room light, the red light in the Theatre was lighted by Walter, to its first or second stage. It is believed that once or twice during the evening he put it out himself; but almost always, he had Butler put it out for him. Usually he lit it himself, though occasionally he had Butler do this too.

There was a prolonged dark interval, followed by a red-light interval, in which the pendulum moved through a wide amplitude, stood steady for a moment in elevated position, etc. Dudley reports a thread-like connection fastened to the projecting mass slightly above the point of suspension, and leading off to the (psychic's) right and down, apparently passing out of the Theater. It was taut when the position of action of the pendulum was such as to suggest that the thread was under tension.

With the scales, after one or two displays without motion in red light, Bird was called upon to put five weights in the west pan, having the option of which pan to use. The next display [i.e., the next time the light in the Theater is switched on] showed this pan inert on the ground. The next showed the pans in substantial static balance. The east pan was strongly tilted, and there was a sharp elbow in one of the suspender threads. Attached to this elbow and running off and down apparently to the lower front east corner of the Theatre, Bird saw a thread-like connection.

The scales performance had been started with the glass front of the Theater raised, to facilitate placing of the weights in the pan. With reference to the fact that he had himself lowered this, Walter now spoke up and said that we had all missed the point of the display. Of course the glass front is seen with difficulty, if at all, in the red light; and we had been concentrating on (looking through it) the scales unit. So none of us observed the condition of the glass front. Bird, however, misinterpreting Walter's remark, asked: "You mean the thread connection, Walter?" Walter said "No," he didn't mean this: and explained what he did mean, giving us a new exposure of red light to show it. *The thread was gone and the pans were normal,* the weighted one grounded. The meaning of Bird's remark had to be explained to Crandon, who then set up the claim that Bird had double control during the levitation of the scales. Walter had to support Bird's correction that this double control had been during the pendulum episode before Crandon would accept it. Double control during the pendulum experiment would be quite as significant as in the scales test.

Walter, during the balance of the sitting, ragged Bird considerably about the thread; Dudley's observation was not known to him. [Dudley had nudged Bird with his elbow in order to signify that he had seen "a thread-like structure"—he had no idea Bird would imagine the thread was not made of ectoplasm!] Toward the end he asked Butler to file off the sharp points of the scales unit—they caught on things. Bird would find a thread hanging on one of them (he said). By implication rather than by direct statement this was connected with the thread seen and reported (during the seance) by Bird. At the end, Bird recovered, from the supporting hook of one suspender cord, a loose bit of blue or black yarn about three inches long. *It was not recovered from the same suspender on which Bird had seen the thread during the seance.*

There was quite a bit of discussion following this revelation, in the middle of the seance, that Bird had seen something described in terms of a thread. Crandon contributed the atmosphere of assuming the object seen to be a thread-like teleplasmic terminal. All sitters fell in with this, and there was nothing said about fraud. Dudley had nudged Bird at the time of making his (own) observation, and took it for granted that Bird had shared his sight of the first thread. Bird had been looking at the ball of the pendulum and hence had missed it. The facts regarding the observation by Dudley became known to the others only after the seance, in the book room. . . .[13]

Bird transcribed these notes the same evening. Curiously enough, instead of then making the matter a subject for an article in the *Journal*, the next morning he mailed the report by registered post to his office at 15 Lexington Avenue, the headquarters of the American Society for Psychical Research. Thus the envelope was postmarked July 16; it was not opened until July 30, 1930, when Bligh Bond and two other society members witnessed the procedure and stated their belief that the envelope had never been opened before.[14]

What was the reason for this curious measure? Bird knew from experience that observers were never readmitted after publishing adverse opinions. It was his belief that some fraud was to be expected in any mediumship and that the occurrence of one carefully controlled supernormal phenomenon was the only thing worth going into print about. To continue searching for such occurrences, Bird was willing to distort and even suppress other facts. So he continued to act as Margery's champion, although appearances in the journal were less frequent; meanwhile he worked quietly on Volume II of the ASPR *Proceedings,* including nearly a hundred pages on the problem of fraud. Yet no word from his prolific typewriter had hinted that Margery was anything but entirely genuine. The public believed in the Margery phenomena largely because of Bird's continuing endorsements; there was no clue that he was telling only half the story.

Meanwhile, Margery moved to new varieties of phenomena in accordance with Walter's expressed wish to become the most versatile control in the history of Spiritualism. Under Richardson's direction, she now attempted to produce trance communications in the form of cross-correspondences. The general arrangement of such phenomena, as studied by the British Society for Psychical Research, is as follows: Medium A is kept from all possibility of contact with Mediums B and C; Medium A communicates in trance an unintelligible message; the only key to the proper understanding of this message is provided by communications from Mediums B and C. Cross-communications are presumably beyond the normal range of telepathic sympathy between subjects; advocates claim they are efforts of surviving spirits to provide a test of their individual identities and of the limits of spiritual interaction with still-embodied souls.

In February 1928, Walter attempted to manifest through Margery, "Dr." Henry Hardwicke of Niagara Falls and George Valiantine—the first medium to apply for the *Scientific American* prize and the first fraud to be exposed by J. Malcolm Bird. Valiantine was a strange cohort. Bird had pronounced against him, and other psychists had and would react similarly. Professor Hans Driesch, noted philosopher and sometime president of the Society for Psychical Research, called his sitting with Valiantine in Berlin in 1929 "the greatest swindle I have ever seen."[15] A participator in the British cross-correspondences, Mrs. W. H. Salter, referred to Valiantine as "thoroughly discredited."[16] Hardwicke was merely one of the countless small fish that Houdini had so delighted in exposing. Mina was becoming less careful. If there is such a thing as guilt by association, she now opened herself to it.

Walter's efforts to communicate partial words, ideographs, and pictures from Lime Street to Hardwicke in Niagara Falls and to Valiantine in New York were marred by the fact that telephone and telegram communication was necessarily open among all parties in order to judge the degree of success.

On February 25, 1928, at 9 P.M., Margery, in trance, drew the face of a clock on a piece of paper. She then wrote the letters TH. At 10:55 P.M., Valiantine "was reported *by phone* [my italics] to have written WAL and drawn the face of a watch." At 11:30 P.M., Crandon received a telegram from Hardwicke, stating that he had drawn something resembling a "circle enclosing an oblique angle," and that he had written the letters MINE.

At the conclusion of the seance a target word and picture selected by Captain Fife was shown to the medium; the word had been WALTHAM and the picture was to be of a "watch-like device for keeping golf-scores."[17] Richardson was correct in supposing that this correspondence of detail was too strong to be coincidence. He also felt, less rightly, that because the medium did not know the word she was supposed to be aiming for, the correspondence could be attributed to supernormal causes. However, the target had been known to the other sitters, who were attempting to play the parts of investigators. One phone call from any member of the circle could have communicated the target from Boston to New York much more effectively than Walter's psychic efforts. No adequate provision had been made against it. Mrs. Salter summarized the situation as she saw it:

> The cross-correspondences, if genuine, argue supernormal powers of an astonishingly high order; in their perfect precision of result they stand unrivalled. Can we suppose such powers to have been shown on some half-a-dozen occasions by a man who has unquestionably resorted

to fraud in the production of physical phenomena,* and whose claim to the possession of any supernormal powers, apart from the cross-correspondences, can be shown to rest upon a most unstable foundation?[18]

Next Margery turned to the "solus sitting." She held one for Dr. R. J. Tillyard of the National Laboratory for Psychical Research, F.R.S., and chief entomologist to the Commonwealth of Australia.[19] The solus sitting, Margery's most significant token gesture to the continued clamor for better controls, put her alone in the seance room with an individual investigator, while another person stood outside the door to preclude confederacy from the outside. Solus sittings were carefully restricted, but Tillyard's happy state of mind in regard to Mina and her work was recommendation enough, and he was speedily admitted.

Margery was seated in the low wooden chair for this seance, which was intended for the production of spirit thumbprints. Tillyard strapped her to the arms of the chair with adhesive tape, which he then marked with blue pencil lines crossing the tape and her wrists to prevent her from freeing and retaping one of her hands. Margery complained that her left wrist was bruised where Walter had earlier taken some teleplasm from her and that the tape hurt her. Tillyard obligingly moved the tape along her forearm above the bruise.[20] V. J. Woolley of the British society wrote later that he felt certain that the tape did not adequately control the movement of Mina's hands; he also believed that the chair was carefully constructed to allow such movements as would be necessary to the fraudulent production of seance-room phenomena.[21] Suppose that Margery had transferred Walter's thumbprint to a cylindrical die* and secreted it within her per-

---

*Mrs. Salter here refers to the evidence published by H. Dennis Bradley in his *—And After*, in which he delineates experiments wherein Valiantine, ambitious to recreate Margery's thumbprint phenomena, left clear prints on paper which were later identified as those of his own big toe.

*Note: As early as 1907, the brilliant detective story writer R. Austin Freeman had published the first of his extremely popular "Dr. Thorndyke" novels, *The Red*

son. Under Tillyard's controls, there was nothing to prevent Margery from withdrawing the die and pressing it into the wax on the table. Tillyard failed to consider the possibility; he was not in the least suspicious when he noted at the end of the sitting that "the bruised area had spread a lot."[22] Small wonder, after such stretching and reaching as would be necessary were the prints he received produced by trickery.

During the sitting, Walter had continually urged Tillyard to inspect Margery's back after the seance, so after the sitting Tillyard asked a young lady to look at Mina's back in the next room. Speaking of himself in the third person, he then went on: "The door was slightly opened; she stated that there was a huge bluish red bruise on Margery's back covering two vertebrae. Dr. Crandon was willing that Tillyard should examine it, but Tillyard said he would be satisfied to see it from the doorway. Miss [Landstrom, the "young lady" mentioned above] then draped Margery and placed her half leaning over a chair, back to the door, with the strong white electric light from the ceiling shining down on her. . . . Tillyard remarked that these were the two vertebrae in his back which had been most badly damaged by arthritis; his own back was feeling immeasurably better. . . ."[23] Of course the psychic element is easily explained if Tillyard had mentioned his arthritic back and if Margery had a convenient bruise on her back already. By taking advantage of the coincidence, Mina could create a most impressive effect. Due to the absence of a thorough preseance examination, this possibility cannot be ignored.

What he failed sufficiently to consider was the fact that Walter's voice had soothed him, possibly employing a kind of hypnosis about which Tillyard does not speak as fully as would be desired,

---

Thumb Mark, in which a method of duplicating thumbprints was explained at considerable length. This method—and others—of print duplication were well known to fingerprint experts by 1926, and we will soon see that the evidence that such duplication had occurred in the Margery phenomena is nearly conclusive.

merely saying that Walter's soothing voice had made him "drowsy."

The entomologist's approach to psychical research is perhaps more interesting. Why would a man of science balk at examining a woman's nude back, especially if her husband was present? Crandon's willingness to display nude photographs of his wife to newsmen suggested bizarre sexual tastes,[24] as did Mina's propensity for talking about her sexual conquests. Did this display remind Tillyard of the many colorful rumors about the Crandons he had heard?

However regrettable Tillyard's technique may have been, his name continued to adorn the list of believers, and European colleagues heard nothing but praise from him about the amazing psychic powers of Margery the medium.

In December 1928, Crandon journeyed alone to England, where he arranged a sitting with Gladys Osborne Leonard, the most famous mental medium then living. Association with a medium of unquestionable honesty, whose trance material was thoroughly verified, would add credibility to the wobbling Margery case. Crandon spoke with Mrs. Leonard's little-girl control, Feda:

Crandon: You are the most famous ghost in the world.
Feda: Yes, isn't it funny? I don't know whether I am as as famous as Walter. I think Walter is a bit famouser.
Crandon: We won't fight on that.
Feda: Walter is saying nothing; isn't he polite? But I think Walter and Feda is famous.
Crandon: Always he has his hat off to Feda.
Feda: Yes, but he is very nice.
Crandon: Feda must look out—he is a great flirt.
Feda: Oh—perhaps he be interesting. When I get outside of her [Mrs. Leonard] I will ask him if he is.
Crandon: Keep your fingers crossed!
Feda: All right; I see about it. Perhaps I won't want to cross them.

Don't forget Feda's love to Margery. Good-bye. God bless you.[25]

Meanwhile, through 1929, Bird was still contributing to the *Journal* such humorous and whimsical pieces as an article, "Chips from the Workshop," in which he discussed the printers' difficulties, his own worries, and a little something about the *Journal*.[26] Then abruptly, in 1930, Bird is seen only twice: once reviewing the medium Wehner's autobiography, *A Curious Life*, for the March issue and last in the following announcement at the end of the 1930 volume:

New York Sectional Activities

The Inaugural Meeting of the autumn Session was held on Monday evening October 20th at Hyslop House. Owing to indisposition, Mr. J. Malcolm Bird was unable to give his advertised address on "Psychical Research and Its Relation with Organized Science." His place was therefore taken by Mr. Bligh Bond who gave an address on "Recent Progress in Psychic Research."[27]

In 1931, the first few numbers of the *Journal* still listed his name as research officer, even though no work by him was published in either 1930 or 1931. And then, without so much as a word of explanation, the name of J. Malcolm Bird disappeared from the *Journal's* cover.

What became of Bird? Where was that long-awaited second volume in the society's history of the Margery mediumship?

For more than thirty-five years, speculation has attributed his separation from the society to everything from personal jealousy to the acceptance of a business opportunity of great promise. Now, with the opening of the Prince file, a wealth of new material has come to light. Because of its significance both to Bird himself and to Margery, I will quote detailed excerpts for the first time.

The first document is the only known extant copy of a paper whose existence was hinted at in 1933 by Prince, writing in the *Scientific American:* "About two years ago . . . he [Bird] sent in to his employers a long paper claiming the discovery of an act of fraud and reconstructing his view of the case to admit a factor of fraud from the beginnning. This paper has not been printed and very few of the believers in Europe or America know of its existence."[28] Nothing more was known of the elements of fraud that Bird had detected; but these selections present, as closely as we are able to reconstruct them, a summary of his new conclusions:

Extracts from the confidential report of Mr. Bird to the Board of Trustees, May 1930

From page 1—The facts being that phenomena normally produced have always impressed me as constituting a small percentage of the total, it has been within my rights to conclude that this aspect of the case was not one of prime importance. It follows that, since May 1924 when I first concluded that the case was one of valid mediumship, my observations have never been directed in any large sense toward the detection of fraud, and even less toward its demonstration. As I went along with my seances, here and there I made, as a matter of routine, observations that some particular episode was normal in its causation. . . .

From page 4—All that the present report aims to do is to acquaint the Board with the date upon which is based in my own mind, the statement which I have made whenever occasion has arisen to make it: that the Margery phenomena are not one hundred per cent supernormal.

From page 6—"A Direct Proposal of Confederacy."—It is not now possible for me to state positively whether the episode occurred in July or in August, 1924. . . . The occasion was one of Houdini's visits to Boston for the purpose of sitting. . . . She sought a private interview with me and tried to get me to agree, in the event that phenomena did not occur, that I would ring the bell-box myself, or produce something else that might pass as activity by Walter. . . .

This proposal was clearly the result of Margery's wrought-up state of mind. Nevertheless it seems to me of paramount importance, in that it shows her, fully conscious and fully normal, in a situation where she thought she might have to choose between fraud and a blank seance; and where she was willing to choose fraud.

From page 7—"Seance-Room Observations Indicating Normal Production of Phenomena."

On April 25, 1924: The table at times, and at time the scales platform, would be tilted; and it became clear that the program involved the initial displacement of the scale pans in this fashion, followed by their maintenance in motion through physical means. . . . Of the initial displacements of the table, three were observed by me to have been produced by normal use of the Psychic's feet; of the platform displacements one was normally produced through use of her elbow. I regarded all other initial displacements as supernormally obtained, as also the extended periods of oscillation of the pans. Margery not in trance.

From page 11—At ten consecutive seances attended by Carrington and Keating in July, 1924, psychic lights were liberally produced. A fraudulent technique here consists in daubing luminous paint on the soles of the stockings. . . . This device can be always detected by cleverly chosen tests that would force an uplifted foot to move. Keating and Carrington reported to me that at times they had positive observations that this technique was being used; and that on other occasions, when it was not, the lights so far as they could judge were valid. These observations are not by me and may properly be objected to as not falling within the scope of the resolution. I mention them because they were made by investigators responsible to me and working for me; and because they imply the use of a premeditated fraud. In this respect they stand almost quite alone, and I should have a certain amount of sympathy for one who rejected them on that basis.

From pages 14 and 15—For July 26, 1925, the statement is made in *Proceedings,* p. 77, that certain manipulations going on the floor would have been evidential only in the presence of a much more severe foot control than the one prevailing. This remark corresponds with my positive observation that the action was got normally. In addition to positive location and identification of the Psychic's right foot, made under cover of my freedom in the room, I was confident that at one stage another foot, from another quarter, was at work. This would have been Dr. Brown, perhaps playing a joke and perhaps testing Walter out as I had done before. He is not to be thought of as a frequent confederate; on numerous grounds this hypothesis may be ruled out. I take it that my own discovery of this evening was in turn observed; for this was the last time I enjoyed the freedom of the room during a seance.

From page 21—Either through Crandon's giving red light a little bit more promptly than one would have expected, or through leakage into the room from without, of sufficient light for accidental silhouetting, or through tactual observation of the location and the direction of extension of the member engaged in the levitation, it has been possible for me to conclude with certainty that an arm or leg of the Psychic was doing duty as a teleplasmic terminal. . . .

Bird's report caused pandemonium in the ranks of the believers despite the general agreement that no medium of the physical type has ever been considered one hundred percent genuine. Bird's explication of that elementary fact of psychical research should have strengthened popular confidence in his critical abilities.

But officials in the society saw that Bird's pronouncement of fraud meant that the society's publication had not told the whole truth, but had suppressed the conclusions of Prince, Hoagland, McComas, and the Rhines, and misrepresented the facts that had been presented.

Bird admitted that in one instance, in the ASPR *Proceedings,* he had written that the phenomena would only be evidential during better foot control, when he really meant that he had detected trickery. Even the most ardent apologist for the case would have had difficulty in explaining how the implication of probable but uncertain genuineness present in the *Proceedings* could really have been meant as an honest effort to report research.

In other words, we now have not merely the accusations and suspicions of Margery's critics, but we also have Bird's gently worded admission that he had been in the practice of telling half-truths, which in science is the same as telling lies.

The personality least affected by Bird's rejection of nearly half the phenomena was Walter. Informed of Bird's announcement, he merely quipped, "Well, if he admits *half* a ghost, that's as good as a *whole* ghost!"[29]

The ASPR could not be so casual. It was clear that the publication of this paper—intended originally to form a portion of the second volume of the ASPR *Proceedings*—would destroy the credibility of the society, which stood or fell with the objective reality of the Margery mediumship. When the officials of the society defended Margery, they were not being gentlemanly. They were engaged in the desperate struggle to preserve what little popular confidence in the ASPR yet remained.

Somehow they had to keep Bird silent and lessen his control on the public dissemination of information. This was why, on the pretext of freeing Bird for more research time, the board appointed Frederick Bligh Bond to the position of editor of the *Journal*.

The society stalled the second volume of the Margery *Proceedings*. In December 1930, seven hundred pages were ready for the board's approval, including the hundred-page analysis of the problem of fraud, which had undergone many forced revisions and complete rewriting.

Despite Bird's efforts to keep his conclusions confidential—having apparently divulged his new findings only to Button and Walton—he received the following anonymous letter "early in May":

My dear Mr. Bird, I have hesitated about writing you this letter and my only excuse is my friendship for the Crandons and my interest in the ASPR.

It would almost seem that in playing the game with Marjorie's enemies, you have played into their hands. I was informed at a tea the other day that a certain man in Boston who had a friend in your Society has finally gotten the Goods on you as he put it. The friend in N.Y. had had you followed, etc. etc. and he claims to have all the data of your private life at his disposal. The Boston man means to publish this in due time, his daughter tells me, and through you, they hope to ruin Marjorie and the ASPR.

It seems that the data has already been given to the Board of directors in N.Y. and they are going to confront you with it. They also mean to tell Mrs. Bird.

The story is told that you are telling that Marjorie asked you to do the so-called psychic happenings and that you are double crossing the whole group with this story. This also has been told to the Board and they maintain if this is true you are to go. The Boston man is just waiting for this to happen to publish the whole thing.

Of course you know any statement will ruin all concerned. I have heard Marjorie say the same thing in a joking way so perhaps that explains it. However this is all true and I only send you this word to be helpful.

Sincerely
J. H.

The story of Bird's alleged indiscretions, as it emerges from the ASPR's archives, is briefly this: Bird, it seems, was seen in the company of a certain unnamed "immoral woman," and had appeared, allegedly quite drunk, with her at Lime Street. Needless to say, the high character of the Crandons did not permit them to admit this woman into the house. Bird at this juncture apparently made some uncharitable remarks about the Crandons' sexual tastes and was peremptorily expelled. This incident, of course, shocked the Crandons, as Bird no doubt ought to have expected. Not only was he denied further admittance to seances, but friends of the Crandons saw no alternative to bringing this episode to the attention of Bird's employers at the ASPR.

In a letter to Prince dated July 29, 1931, Bird sheds the following light on this accusation: "They [the Board] are aware that they are suppressing important evidence, and they can satisfy their consciences only by making themselves believe that the witness who offers this evidence is unworthy of belief. I shall be neither surprised nor aggrieved at anything they do in this direction, after they have gone to the length of trying to make it appear that my frequent Boston trips were the cloak for a series of illicit amours."

Bird shortly thereafter completed the *Proceedings* and placed them in the hands of the Board of Publications, deleting any mention of the seance of July 15, 1927. This enormous output of labor was never published; in all likelihood it was destroyed, as careful searches in the files of the ASPR have failed to disclose any trace of it. Its loss may or may not be attributed to the absence of the one objective individual on the board: on December 22, 1930, Dr. George H. Hyslop tendered his resignation from the board of the American Society for Psychical Research, which his father had founded and to which he had felt a family loyalty until the Margery case eradicated all of the high evidential standards his father had labored to establish.

Bird, determined to see his work published, offered it to the BSPR. Following consultation with his council, Prince decided against publication of the paper. Although it is evident from his letters that he favored letting Bird's criticisms see the light, the majority of the officials felt that the best policy was to ignore the Margery affair altogether. In its sordid involutions and scandalous complications, the case was already recognized as dominating the darkest era in the history of psychical research.

Even the British society, separated as it was from the intimate involvement of the Boston organization, refused to print Bird's paper.

In December 1930, to the surprise of none and the delight of many, Bird resigned from the society. His years of fierce defense of Mina Crandon had contributed perhaps more than any other factor to public belief in her phenomena, but his style of defense ultimately degraded the society from a scientific organization to a forum for character assassination of all who refused to believe in the great Margery.

After some brief discussions with Prince concerning the possibility of presenting his paper at the next International Congress, Bird disappeared from psychical research. On December 8, 1932, after having "spent a day with him," Prince whimsically remarked to a correspondent: "Really, and peculiarly, I have not the least idea what Bird has been doing for the last two years. There was no reference to his occupation during my short stay in his home. My secretary here suggests that he may be 'bootlegging,' but this suggestion is not to be taken seriously. . . ."

For five years I have made every possible attempt to learn what became of Bird, but every lead has become a dead end. To all intents and purposes, Bird, disillusioned and embittered, seems to have broken every connection with his past before retiring into a mysterious obscurity.

How can his contribution to the history of psychical research be evaluated? He was an apologist at best and a backbiter at worst; he was motivated by a keen interest in the reality of supernormal phenomena at the same time that he was willing to lie to convince others of that reality. It was he who was responsible for Margery's fame—it was even he who christened her with her *nom du seance*. That he should suffer the consequences of his own propagandist program when he himself wished to discuss fraud is indeed ironic. But no more poetically just touch could have been added by any writer of fiction than that contributed by the facts: the day he met Mina she had just heard an accusation of fraud, centered about a piece of yarn or a raveling from a rug, while Bird's ultimate disillusionment with Margery stemmed from his observation of a bit of yarn attached to the chemical scales.

Thus it was that James Malcolm Bird had begun his association with the bewitching, enigmatic woman whose effect on him changed his life and the course of psychical research—an association that began and ended with a piece of string.

XVI

The Great Exposure

THERE IS NO DOUBT that Bird and his approach to psychical research did immeasurable harm to any claim it had as a scientific discipline. But at the same time, it was not science that the Margery case needed, it was believers. Believers were essential to spread the word that Walter had proven his identity, to tell the world that psychic phenomena were repeated at will and abundantly verified. And for this, a scientific approach would have been inimical. Dudley, for instance, was extremely exacting in his classifications of the Walter thumbprints, but he was unbelievably lax in his seance control procedures. So that while there was an impressive orderliness about the thumbprints, their supernormality was still in question.

Meanwhile, Mina was at last beginning to lose her attractiveness to men. Photographs taken during the thirties show that she was gaining weight and beginning, not only to show her age, but to look older than she was.

In some ways it did not matter, however: Button was extravagantly devoted to her, both as a woman and as a medium. He was a dear friend to her when she most needed one, and he was an experienced lawyer, which enabled him to defend her honor and her mediumship with impressive ardor. On the ASPR Board of Trustees now were included Walton, Richardson, Pierson, and several others, all of whom were personal friends of the Crandons, and several of whom were in some measure indebted to

Margery for their belief in survival after death.

The society supported Margery as the last and greatest link with an unseen world; they had nearly all become, by now, convinced Spiritualists, and Margery was their somewhat battle-worn messiah. And to keep excitement fluttering about her, without letting any new unbelievers into the circle, Margery on occasion required help from "normal" means.

One way in which she enlarged her sphere was through the assistance of Mrs. Sary Litzelmann, a long-time friend and herself a medium whose lesser light was often lost beside the multitalented Mina Crandon. Sary often produced automatically written mirror messages that served as a poor man's cross-correspondence with something Walter was saying through Margery. If these two ladies did not collaborate on these simple tests, then they certainly did things the hard way for no clear reason; the tests would never satisfy an objective observer in any case. During the physical seances, there is some evidence of collusion. Richardson reports that during a seance (September 23, 1930), he detected Sary's hand moving correspondingly with the sounds of a tilting and creaking cabinet behind Margery's chair. Of course, he believed that Sary was undergoing a sympathetic rather than a causative process.[1]

One investigation, which Richardson considered "the first *independent* evidence of the survival of the individual marks of personality in permanent record under absolute test conditions,"[2] was called "The Judge's Sign Manual."

Charles Stanton Hill was one of the authors of *Margery-Harvard-Veritas* and a votary at Margery's altar. He was a lawyer who was called Judge simply as a gesture of respect. Hill died on the second of September 1930, after having left his own fingerprints in wax with the dubious Captain Fife. If he found himself able to do so, he meant to leave postmortem prints through Margery.

Hill's first incorporeal appearance at Lime Street occurred on September 8, when raps identified his presence. He promised, as soon as he became accustomed to his new environment, to give them his teleplasmic prints. On September 23, a sitting was held in which Walter came through, although he had been absent from Lime Street for nearly two months. Some raps came from Hill's still unfamiliar spirit, and then Walter announced, "No more sittings this week." But when the lights were turned on, both Sary Litzelmann and Margery were entranced and unable to be awakened. Richardson describes the events that followed:

> Then, in the midst of profound silence (no circle), Margery rose to her feet and with eyes tightly closed and hands in front of her, walked around the west end of the table in front of Sherburne, and put her two hands on the sides of his head. He was standing, but Margery pushed him into his chair. She then tore off all the red paper from the side light, tore it into two masses and put one in Sary's left hand. As Margery returned to her seat one of her feet dragged as the Judge's foot did after his stroke. [Lighting a match, Margery burned the red paper on a glass table.] As it burned, she stood and bowed over it very profoundly seven times using hand gestures known to Mr. Litzelmann (from his occult studies) but not to Margery or the rest of us.[3]

It was evident to Richardson that Mina was "possessed" of Judge Hill's spirit. And it is clear to us (if it was not before) that the observers were no longer psychical researchers, but mere occultists. Nonetheless, Richardson felt some responsibility to design an experiment to assure at least a scientific appearance. This is the procedure he suggested to Walter on November 3:

> I would bring to a sitting ten calendar numbers (properly marked for identification) in two series to match the ten fingers: R1, R2, R3, R4, R5 —L1, L2, L3, L4, L5. From these ten numbers (properly shuffled) a single number would be chosen (in the dark) and shown to Walter (in the dark). The Judge should then produce the print suggested by the number thus fortuitously chosen. [The reader must remember that Walter reads in the dark without difficulty.]
> With such a procedure it is plain that the use of dies would require

(a) that Margery smuggle into the seance room ten dies; (b) that she read the chosen number in the dark; (c) that she pick the proper die in the dark; and (d) that she impress the die upon the wax in the dark even though both hands were adequately held.[4]

We will grant that this sounds pretty good; the possibility of all these things being effected seems too remote for consideration. Let us now turn to the design as it operated in the actual sitting of November 7:

Circle: Margery, Dr. Richardson, Mr. Button, Harriet Richardson, J. W. Fife (Fingerprint Expert), Patty Richardson, Mr. Dudley, Mrs. Richardson, Mr. Litzelmann, Mrs. Litzelmann, and Dr. Crandon. Outside circle: R. G. Adams and B. K. Thorogood.

Sitting began at 8:55 P.M. Trance very deep, interval between respirations occasionally as long as seventy seconds. After some preliminary conversation Walter asked me [Dr. Richardson] to bring out my two series of numbers. For identification each number was marked on the back by the print of my right thumb. At Walter's request the numbers, properly shuffled, were placed upon the table for Walter's inspection. After this had been carried out the numbers were given to Mr. Fife with the instruction that he should count them. This he did but could find only eight slips. Fife then chose from the eight a single number and placed it on the table. In a few minutes Walter placed this slip in my hand and I turned it over to Mr. Button who put it in his pocket. The remaining seven slips were given into the custody of Mr. Dudley.

Walter then asked for hot water and the usual procedure was carried out. Wax properly identified by Thorogood and later on by Dudley was placed in the hot water. In a few moments the print was heard to splash in the [pan of] cold water and was removed by Fife. Walter then said that Hill had made his print "and now he is going back to sleep and you won't hear much from him for some time."

Sitting closed at 10:45 P.M. Search was then made for the two missing slips, and one was found on the floor under the northwest corner of the table and the other was on Margery's chair.

It must be understood that all the fingerprint procedure was carried out in absolute darkness. Downstairs, in bright light Mrs. Litzelmann

wrote something in mirror writing and stated that this writing desig-
nated accurately the number on the slip held by Button. Fife and
Dudley examined the wax and made a preliminary diagnosis of the
Judge's left thumb. . . .
    At the sitting of November 10th Button for the first time disclosed
that the slip consigned to him was marked L1. Litzelmann then said
that the mirror writing of Mrs. Litzelmann also stated that the print
was L1.[5]

This test was thought by the group to constitute proof not only
of supernormal exteriorization of energy but also of Judge Hill's
survival. The report is typical of the standards of evidence accept-
able to the American Society for Psychical Research, which was
now lamentably restricted to the believers. It is often cited as an
airtight verification of spirit survival. Nandor Fodor, in his *Ency-
clopedia of Psychic Sciences,* characterizes "the Judge's Sign Manual"
in only slightly more restrained terms. Let us see how well the
experiment escapes the possibility of fraud.

The prints that Hill made during his lifetime were in the files
of Captain Fife. We are not told when he received them. Was it
a day later, or a week, after Hill's death? Had the Crandons had
time to make a die from these prints again, supposing that such
a die could be made? Do we know enough about the mysterious
Fife to exclude the possibility that he assisted in such a scheme?
We may assume that there were several ways for Margery to
obtain dies made from all the prints Hill left. In any case, the lack
of precautions taken to avoid such a likelihood make the report
weak beyond the point where we should be required to take it
seriously.

But, on the assumption that Margery did have the dies, the rest
of the report comports quite well with the theory of fraud. Consider the first point in Richardson's design: that Margery would
have to smuggle in ten dies. As the procedure was actually
effected in the sitting of November 7, this would not have to be
the case. The numbered slips were first presented to Walter for

his inspection. When they were then counted, only eight remained. Richardson supposes that the other two had merely fallen to the floor, but we may suppose that Walter retained them. All that Walter would have had to do was to select the slip that matched *one* die already in the possession of Margery or a confederate within the circle. The other missing slip was pure ornamentation. Thus, when Fife placed the target slip on the table, Walter needed only to substitute the slip he had retained, dropping the actual target on the floor. Of course, Fife did not know which slip he placed on the table, and so could not have detected any such substitution.

With a dab of luminous paint on the inside of her robe or a small pocket flashlight secreted beneath a piece of heavy cloth, Margery could look through the slips of paper and select the one that matched a die. Fifteen ASPR officials had been taken in by a similar ruse in 1927, when McComas staged his own seance. That they should be so fooled again is certainly not beyond the limits of probability.

How could she impress the die in the warm wax "even though both her hands were adequately held"? But Crandon readily admitted to his habit of relinquishing control of his wife's hand during seances.

From the skeptic's standpoint, the Richardson report almost describes each step in the fraud. If Richardson may be excused on the grounds that he thought Mina incapable of trickery, the others cannot be so lightly absolved. They were foolish as well as naïve, but their work filled the new *Journal of the ASPR* for all the world to read and wonder.

Other changes were taking place in the *Journal.* Aside from featuring discussions of astrology and cabalistic rites, it was, by 1931, displaying a decidedly spiritistic trend. The articles were uncritical and the analyses shallow. Much space was now devoted to enthusiastic discussions of metaphysics and religion. For several months, articles by "William James and the S.P.R. Group," under the heading of *Discarnate Knowledge,* had been communicating facts about the spirit world. These incredible documents were included without editorial comment, and only readers who had followed the series knew that the authors were the *spirits* of James, Myers, and other figures of psychic fame who had been dead for years. There was even a postmortem contribution by Charles Darwin!

Then, in February 1931, William H. Button was elected president of the ASPR. He was now to share with Richardson the dubious honor of being the major chronicler of the Lime Street work. Dudley, meanwhile, pored over the collected thumbprints of all who had ever attended a Margery seance, comparing them carefully with the prints Walter proclaimed as his own. While engaged in this work, Dudley was financed by the generous Crandon, as it had "developed that he was somewhat needy financially."[6] Articles from his energetic pen were seen frequently in the *Journal.*

All of this must have given Mina the distinct feeling that she had it made. She was the center of the most devoted clique ever to surround a medium since the days of D. D. Home, and she possessed as well the personal and the official favor of William Button.

Button was fifty-nine, wealthy, successful, and an altogether desirable person to have on one's side. His weaknesses were occultism and his consequent belief in human survival of bodily death. About science he knew next to nothing.

According to an article in the *New York Times* of May 6, 1944, Button was a corporation lawyer admitted to the bar in 1890. He was a graduate of Middlebury and an active member of the Union League Club, the University Club, the Lawyers Club, and the India House in New York; in Washington, he belonged to the Cosmos Club. During 1934 he made $41,504 for his legal services. He was married and had two daughters and a son. His wife attended the Lime Street sittings and, despite rumors that can still be heard, there is no evidence that Margery came between them. It was all one, big, bizarre, but happy, family.

So it was that Richardson, working on his manuscript in 1947, was able to reflect nostalgically on those fine days when "the American Society for Psychic Research, under the leadership of its president, Mr. William H. Button, supported the mediumship to the utmost."[7]

The quality of Button's psychical research may be judged from his report of a solus sitting on March 10, 1931. It was a sitting for prints, so Button exercised great care in his control measures: he first taped Margery's fingers and wrists to the arms of the chair, then locked the door to the seance room and stationed Richardson to prevent the entry of an accomplice. The innocent Button said he "would not have thought of" these precautions but Walter suggested them. Button was rewarded for his efforts with another fine Walter thumbprint.[8]

Walter, meanwhile, was exploring other avenues of expression. For many years he had been producing poetry through the automatic writing of his sister, such as this bitter quatrain written after a visit to the skeptical Society for Psychical Research during the year 1929:

> *To the S.P.R.*
>
> Good-bye to ye—we bid ye all farewell,
> The clarion calls—the ghosts in haste depart.
> We will no longer bide within your walls,
> We'll view ye from afar—ye S.P.R.
> (Feb. 17, 1930)

At one time Crandon had a pamphlet of Walter's poetry published, but by and large, there was nothing in them beyond the reasonable efforts of Mina's conscious mind. One poem, however, stands out among the others for its expression of a deeper mood. It was composed on May 7, 1931, on the death of Mother Stinson:[9]

In Majesty Death Comes

In majesty death comes:
He walks alone,
Comes here as your friend.
Why weep? You'd have it so.
He knows you know 'tis not the end.

As with a perfect day:
The sun has set.
With gracious hand he gives ˏyou perfect peace.
They answer his great call:
They find release.

Ah! Majesty, we worship at thy throne.
Thy will be done: the power,
We do believe.
God, give us strength
To know and feel and not to grieve.

While Walter was engaging himself with his little miracles, another schism began to develop within the already badly torn society. It seems that Dudley himself was growing disenchanted. Dudley had taken an energetic part in the low-level defense of Margery's honor that appeared in the Spiritualist *Banner of Life* following the Rhine report; his uncritical pen was so warmly appreciated that he actually pursued his "investigation" under Crandon's beneficent employ.

Beyond that, it may be said that Dudley was a disheveled little man whose unruly gray hair had a way of bristling in several directions, while his drooping gray moustache served only to accentuate the dull expression of his mouth and the weakness of his chin.

Bird had been shown unworthy of public confidence in his observational abilities, and Dudley came into his own. This curious victory at once disarmed an attack and cut off much of the previous defense of the case.

In the autumn of 1929, Dudley introduced the Crandons to a man with the most Pickwickian of names, Brackett K. Thorogood, Dudley's new assistant.

Thorogood attended the Chauncey Hall School in Boston and the Massachusetts Institute of Technology. "He practiced his profession for twenty years," Richardson tells us, "and for ten years was Instructor in the Mechanical Engineering Department of the Graduate School of Engineering of Harvard University, from which he resigned to take charge of the rehabilitation and training of ex-service men as Educational Counsellor at the Franklin Union, a technical institute in Boston. . . . For more than thirty years Mr. Thorogood has pursued the study of abnormal psychology—and psychic phenomena as an avocation."[10] In June 1931, Thorogood was appointed to the specially created post of research consultant.

The post should have been Dudley's. He had, after all, studied the prints in greater detail than anyone else, he had been there longer than most of the current believers, and he had devoted considerable effort to rewriting Bird's enormous mass of material. But somewhere along the line Crandon had decided that Dudley did not suit his needs as exactly as Thorogood. With characteristic abruptness, Crandon had determined to place Thorogood in complete control of Margery's seances.

Dudley was understandably piqued. He now began to find himself less welcome. The climax of the situation came when Dudley found a lock on the seance room, placed there by Crandon to protect Thorogood's apparatus. As Dudley later complained, "I found myself forced out."[11]

Perhaps Crandon knew that Dudley was on a dangerous track that would one day lead him to make uncomfortable discoveries about Walter and his invisible thumb. From the beginning, Dudley had compared Walter's prints with those of every sitter present at the seances. What he thought he had established—and what the society wished others to believe—was that this last fact proved the presence of "someone" else in the seance room. Now Dudley began to compare Walter's prints with those of every sitter who had attended a Lime Street seance *before* his arrival on the scene. When he began contacting Bird's list of sitters for 1923–1924, he found himself less welcome than before.

Meanwhile, Walter had performed the amazing feat of reproducing in Lime Street the astral thumprints of Sir Oliver Lodge while he was peacefully asleep across the Atlantic. Walter explained that these were prints of Sir Oliver's etheric double (or materialized spirit), summoned by occult powers from the unconscious body of the famous physicist. These incredible experiments took place under Thorogood's auspices on July 13, 14, and 15, 1931.[12]

Other problems were developing within the society. In 1929, after observing Margery perform at a private seance in London, Harry Price, the foreign research officer of the ASPR, wrote to Theron Pierce of the Board of Trustees,

It is obvious to every psychist in this country, that the policy of the American SPR is rapidly changing. When, in 1925, I consented to represent the Society in Europe, I felt that under its new Research Officer, experiments of a scientific nature would be carried out and that its reports would attract the attention of official science. . . . But what has happened is this: the American Society for Psychical Research is now in the grip of the spiritualists, and the stranglehold of the Crandon party —on both sides of the Atlantic—is slowly but surely throttling the life out of it. . . . Were it not for its fine journal . . . with its important foreign contributors, the American S.P.R. would have no particular reason for continuing its existence. . . . I am thoroughly sympathetic with the tenets and philosophy of the spiritualistic religion, but "faith" had no connection whatever with scientific research. . . . My sincere and disinterested advice to the American S.P.R. is: get clear of the "Margery" case before the crash comes. . . ."[13]

In 1930, Price felt compelled to resign his office, for which he had never received any impressive remuneration; and by 1931 his featured "International Notes," which had graced the last seventy-one months of the *Journal,* were terminated.[14]

In Price's usual spot, Bligh Bond now published his editorial effusions and gallant affirmations of faith in Margery's subjective trance material. He informs us in one issue that the "Winnipeg Mediumship"—begun in Canada a few months before—had succeeded in opening communications with Walter.[15]

Margery was not idle, either. A gifted Irish trance medium, Eileen Garrett, had crossed the Atlantic to be studied by American investigators. Margery had a seance with her on November 5, 1931. In February 1932, Mina had the happy-go-lucky audacity to submit her "report" on Mrs. Garrett's mediumship to the *Journal,* which gladly printed it.

Walter, Mina tells us, came through in all his usual splendor, saying such things as: "Thank God I don't sing. Well, Kid, you certainly are an old fraud, but I am in on it. Never mind, let them think what they like."[16] The irony of Mina posing as an investigator is made more amusing by hindsight: we now know that Mrs. Garrett was a uniquely gifted woman whose mediumship was richly endowed with genuine supernormal knowledge and whose gifts were subjected to the most exacting study. One of her most careful investigators was Dr. J. B. Rhine, now of the psychology department of Duke University, where he was already analyzing the data for the reality of extrasensory perception.

In 1932, Button was again elected to the presidency of the society. "I accepted this office," he told readers of the *Journal,* "because of my conviction that the work of the Society is of the utmost importance and also because the phenomena with which it deals are the most fascinating in the world."[17]

Among his projects was a seemingly very well done test of Walter's clairvoyant powers. Button constructed a heavy box, capable of being locked and sealed, into which he placed a number of objects known only to him. Walter told him with precision what each one was. Such tests are often found even today among questionable mediums, and their success depends on unscrewing and then reassembling the bottom of the box. Button's test box does not, in all fairness, seem amenable to this technique.

By this time Margery was far from careful about the ways she gained her successes. Eileen Garrett told me on April 13, 1967, of several instances when Mina called her on the phone with offers of assistance at Mrs. Garrett's seances. On one occasion, before a sitting with some prestigious New Yorkers, Mrs. Garrett received a call from Margery offering to tell the secrets of the sitters, by way of professional cooperation. Although Mrs. Garrett repeatedly rejected these overtures, Margery told with relish how she supplied information by way of innocent conversation to the famous British medium. The rumors nearly succeeded in seriously damaging Mrs. Garrett's reputation in this country. Nonetheless, Mina's personality was so engaging that Mrs. Garrett could never really resent her: "She was probably the most utterly charming woman I have ever known." Although Mrs. Garrett's opinion was that Margery's phenomena at this period were produced by fraud and collusion, it was somehow difficult to resent her lighthearted destruction of American psychism.

It was into this placid, happy scene that, in March 1932, a revelation exploded like a bomb, shaking the very foundations of the cause.

One evening Dudley returned from the office of Dr. Frederick Caldwell, Margery's dentist, who had first suggested using dental wax for the digital impressions; he settled down to routinely inspect the fingerprints he had obtained during the week from people on his 1923–1924 list of sitters. Then he saw it. He examined both sets of prints to be sure, but there was no mistake. *The thumbprints, both right and left, that Walter had been announcing as his own since 1926, were identical in every respect with Dr. Caldwell's!*

Attempting to quell his amazement, Dudley counted no less than twenty-four absolute correspondences.

The next day, he went to Caldwell's offices again and asked him point-blank if he recalled giving his prints to Mina. Seeing that there was trouble afoot, Caldwell refused to answer Dudley's questions until he called Margery. What she told him is not known, but Caldwell's cooperation was not forthcoming.

Dudley realized that he did not require any admission from Caldwell; he had enough evidence to convict a criminal. He communicated to Button his desire to alter the second volume of the *Proceedings,* which was now in manuscript form and ready to print. He did not specify the nature of the alterations, although he guaranteed that they would not be extensive. But Caldwell's phone call to Margery had let the cat out of the bag, and Button was aware of the probable nature of Dudley's discovery.

In a letter to Button dated March 18, 1932, Dudley expressed the case succinctly:

In my letter of March 11th, I stated that I had obtained additional evidence in connection with the finger-print matter which would necessitate certain textual changes. This consists of the identification of the right and left thumb prints known as "the Walter Prints," with the thumb prints of a living person, one of the early sitters in Lime Street seances. After these had been enlarged and analyzed I took them to competent experts who agreed that the identification was unusually complete. . . . Two things are proved: three-dimensional prints of normal form can be successfully duplicated; and the "Walter" prints are not those of Walter Stinson, deceased. Therefore, the prints of a living person have been made since the beginning of the experiments.

Button expressed his surprise, but he was not convinced, as he later assured readers of the *Journal:* "The problem was presented to 'Walter' and he immediately ridiculed the idea that his prints were identical with Mr. X's."[18] Fortified by this, Button asked Dudley on March 21: "Why should Walter select the print of a living man to produce all these years?"

Dudley seems to have believed at this point that not all the thumbprints produced by Walter were fraudulent. In a letter dated March 24, he assured Button that the supernormality of the prints would stand or fall on the conditions of control under which they were obtained.

From a strictly scientific standpoint identification has very little bearing on the question of supernormal versus normal origin. You raise the question as to why "Walter" selected the prints of someone else. I do not know. That is up to him. There are plenty of puzzles in pyschical research. This is another one. It may be solved later; or it may not. At present it is just an inescapable fact.

He defined his position more clearly in a letter on the twenty-seventh:

Dear Mr. Button,

Margery informs me that you are not satisfied with my letter of the 24th, and that you want me to make a direct positive statement that the fingerprints are of supernormal origin.

I have never controlled the course of these finger print experiments, never occupied the position of control while they were being made, nor had a solus sitting. The prints were made in darkness, therefore, I am dependent on the statements of others as to most of their actions, and these statements I must take on faith, as must the reader of the reports. If these statements are unreservedly accepted it would appear that a considerable number of the prints were made supernormally. I have testified to my part in these sittings, and to my knowledge as to what others have or have not done. Beyond that I cannot properly go. . . .

I have shown that certain prints would be difficult of production by normal means. I think no one would claim that such production would be *impossible*. . . .

Sincerely yours,
E. E. Dudley

Margery's reliability as a medium of even normal communication was questionable, as Button's reply of March 28 demonstrates:

In yours of the 27th you say that Margery has informed you that I was dissatisfied with your letter of the 24th and wished you to make a direct statement to the effect that the finger prints produced at Lime Street are supernormal. This is entirely incorrect. Margery informed me that you had told her at great length that despite your recent information it was your opinion that all the prints obtained at Lime Street were supernormal and that anybody but a fool would know it. I told Margery that if that was your position, I wished you would write me that instead of the noncommittal position you have taken in your . . . letters. . . ."

Dudley clarified this on the 31st by saying: "I told her it was foolish, even absurd, to assume that Caldwell had anything to do with the making of the seance-room prints . . . it was obvious that such a man would have no part in deceit. She then advanced this proposition: He did not make the prints (seance room); she knew that she did not make them, therefore they must have been supernormal. This is such illogical reasoning that it seemed to require no comment. . . ." This was Dudley's first disclosure of the possessor of the so-called Walter thumbprints.

The decision was made to delay all discussion of the thumbprint evidence that was already in the second volume of the *Proceedings*. A third volume would examine the problem exclusively. Dudley nonetheless wrote an article dealing with the evidence; for clarity, conciseness, and logic, it was the best thing he ever did. Giving Caldwell the pseudonym Kerwin, he submitted the paper to the *Journal* and received the following note, dated July 6, 1932,

Dear Sir,

By direction of the Research Committee of the A.S.P.R. I would inform you that the Society does not care to publish your article on the Walter-Kerwin fingerprint subject for the reason, among others, that the Committee is not satisfied with the identity of the prints involved as maintained by you.

I understand that a statement in reference thereto will appear in the July number of the Journal. I will return the article to you when I get back to New York.

Very sincerely,
American Society for Psychical Research,
By Wm. H. Button, Pres.

Dudley was not daunted by this. He communicated the situation to Dr. Walter Franklin Prince at the Boston Society for Psychic Research. Prince was thunderstruck at Button's audacity in refusing to publish one of the most important studies of any single seance phenomenon in the history of the case. Fearing the ASPR would suppress this report as it had suppressed those of Hoagland, Code, McComas, the Rhines, Bird, and even his own review, Prince decided to sponsor Dudley's article for publication as a Boston society *Bulletin*. The members of the Boston council agreed that it was even more conclusive than Bird's long paper; it was therefore published as the *Bulletin of the Boston Society for Psychic Research*, Volume 18, October 1932.

This article—by the man who refused even to see the cogency of Bird's evidence of fraud, who was employed by the society for the purpose of discrediting Bird as an observer, and who was, before this discovery, one of Margery's most energetic supporters—created near-pandemonium when it was published. Thorogood was instructed by the research committee to do what he could to combat the charges; meanwhile, Button submitted the enlargements of the prints to Dr. Harold Cummins of the department of anatomy of Tulane University for his opinion.

Thorogood and Button at last voiced the conclusion—expanded in Thorogood's *The Margery Mediumship III: The "Walter" Hands*—that Dudley, either through neglect or for reasons known best to him, had substituted the real Walter prints with those made from dies of Caldwell's prints. Although this is a simplification of the argument, the report was far from complimentary to Dudley. It accused him of harboring deep-seated resentments toward the Crandons and the society for excluding him from a controlling position and intimated that Dudley sought to discredit the case due to this thwarted ambition. But beyond this, Thorogood attempted to fight the charge with new evidence—an almost unique method for the society in recent years.

He analyzed the early paraffin gloves and found that their

thumbprints did not match Caldwell's. Thorogood suggested that the gloves were so incompletely documented as to afford little assurance that the prints really were Walter's and that what Dudley calls the "standard" Walter print actually was standard. New experiments were conducted to obtain a set of prints established as Walter's. These new prints varied significantly from the Caldwell prints under a microscope. Such was Thorogood's defense.

It as all in vain: one final blow, delivered from across the Atlantic, shattered all attempts to discredit Dudley's discovery.

The opinion requested from Cummins had arrived in time to be included in Thorogood's report. Cummins, who knew nothing of the controversy and was consulted only for his expertise in fingerprint identification, was of the opinion that the "Walter" print and that of "Kerwin" were absolutely identical.[19] Perhaps Button and his friends saw no alternative to publishing this adverse report, because it was in fact printed. It was surrounded, however, by the criticisms of Thorogood, mechanical engineer and amateur abnormal psychologist. He had made a crash study of fingerprint science and concluded that Cummins was mistaken and biased against psychic phenomena.

A few months after the *Proceedings* came out, the Boston Society for Psychic Research published its *Bulletin* entitled: "The 'Walter'-'Kerwin' Thumb Prints." In this volume, Cummins analyzed the attack made upon his competency. He did not engage in personal abuse (such as had been leveled against him), but again went over the specific items of identification. His conclusions were: (1) The right and left thumbs of "Walter" were identical with those of "Kerwin"; (2) those prints that included both the palms and the prints of "Walter" were composites: the thumbs were "Kerwin's" while the palms were those of an unknown individual; and (3) it is a "simple process" to make dies precisely suitable for the fraudulent production of any subject's fingerprint.[20] In this opinion he was supported by Inspector W. T. Bell of Scotland Yard, who informed the ASPR that dies of a person's fingerprints could be made after only a short meeting. He added that he believed the Oliver Lodge prints could have been made in this way during Crandon's visits to England in 1929. Thus a promising test of Walter's powers was discredited and no one spoke very loudly of the Lodge prints afterward.[21]

Even Frederick Bligh Bond was shaken by Cummins's first report. On December 31, 1933, when Thorogood's work of apology had just appeared, Bond wrote in a private letter:

> Things at Hyslop House are going more crazily than ever and now I am called upon as Editor to publish an article by our president on the old "Margery" business of the thumb prints, and I cannot refuse to do so, though I am ashamed to have to sponsor its appearance even to this extent. It is sheer nonsense—not in any sense a scientific document but a piece of special pleading and to my mind very weak and lacking in any feeling of sincerity. But I hear that our Board are determined to pursue their course of "vindicating" this mediumship and have arranged for another year's investigation and retained the services of their research man for the whole of 1934 for this purpose, making his fee a first charge on the fund for our endowment. Meanwhile our home resources at Hyslop House are strained, our salaries cut, and all clerical help denied. We have not even an office boy to answer the door.[22]

The final crisis in the Margery case was the publication of a third report from Cummins early in 1935. It was printed by the Society for Psychical Research, that bastion of conservative silence during the half-decade of most heated debate regarding the Margery case.

It seems that Margery had not exercised sufficient care about the distribution of her brother's thumbprints. On December 7, 8, and 9, 1929, the seance room of the London society was used for demonstration sittings by the visiting Dr. and Mrs. Crandon. Present, among others, were Dr. V. J. Woolley (then research officer of the society), Mrs. Eve Brackenbury (also of the society), and the persistent Harry Price, who had insisted on being given a Margery seance in spite of Crandon's reluctance to allow the renowned ghostbreaker a place. Woolley and Price were each rewarded with a Walter thumbprint, and it was this indiscretion on Walter's part that now came back to haunt him.

Dr. Harold Cummins happened to be in London in the summer of 1934, when he met with W. H. Salter, one of the best-known members of the London society. Salter mentioned to Cummins that the society's secretary had recently come into possession of a key, kept by Woolley until his resignation. The key opened a box in which Woolley had stored the ghost's thumbprint after the sitting of December 7, five years before.

Salter and Cummins were equally eager to have another look at this print: if it could be shown to be a Caldwell print, then there could be no doubt that Dudley had not substituted any prints out of a spirit of vindictiveness toward the ASPR and Margery, and that Walter had, for eight years, been using Frederick Caldwell's print as his own.

On August 1, 1934, Cummins opened the box and examined the impression in the presence of Miss Newton, Salter, and Stanley de Brath (a Margery believer who had been invited to bring along a Walter print from the British College of Psychic Science, a Spiritualist "laboratory"). In addition to the prints supplied by Woolley and de Brath, Cummins inspected two Walter thumbs sent for the purpose by Lord Charles Hope.[23] Later, he was able to examine three prints owned by Professor F. C. S. Schiller, dated September 9, 10, and 11, 1929. All these impressions had been untouched for five years.

And all of them, unquestionably, were the thumbprints of Dr. Frederick Caldwell of Boston.[24]

The Crandon party never replied adequately to this evidence. Here was no case of an investigator saying he saw one thing, while a Margery advocate claimed to have seen another; the evidence was clear and permanent, and no rebuttal would have been of the least use.

Within a few days of Cummins's discovery, Walter Franklin Prince died, at the age of seventy-one. He was (if anyone in this incredible affair was) the hero of the Margery case. Through his efforts to acquaint the public with facts that might otherwise have been suppressed, he provided a forum for the most significant criticism of the case. He also published the many positive studies that culminated in 1934 in the publication of J. B. Rhine's *Extra-Sensory Perception,* the book that would reshape the future of psychical research.

In full appreciation of the course he steered in those hysterical years, years so crucial to the history of psychic science, we conclude this chapter with Prince's estimate of this last great exposure, written to Joe Rinn on February 1, 1934,[25] "Now, in my judgment, the Margery case will, in time, come to be considered the most ingenious, persistent, and fantastic complex of fraud in the history of psychic research."

XVII

The End of an Era

MINA CRANDON's last years are poorly documented. With the death of Prince, the last private file ceased to be compiled, leaving only occasional shadows between the lines of the reports that continued to fill the pages of the ASPR *Journal.*

With Button in his sixties and Mina in her forties, their riotous friendship grew closer as these last hectic years wore on. In the thirties Walter summoned up renewed energy, thus keeping Margery and her stalwart investigators busy.

Some of the phenomena during this period were palpably ridiculous; others were so mysterious that many intelligent people continue to feel that an element of the mediumship was genuine. Disbelief, as well as belief, is a state of mind in which emotions play a large part; and the Margery case was noted for the heated emotions it aroused on both sides.

Richardson, Margery's best and truest friend, was caught up with the problem of his two sons' survival to the point where his sagacity was affected. He never thought for a minute that the personalities of his two friends warranted any real consideration of fraud.

There was some justification for the annoyance Richardson and others felt with the dogmatic disbeliever. Many who wrote with apparent authority about the falseness of the mediumship had never been granted a single sitting. If fraud was not evidenced in the seance reports, it was assumed that the fraud occurred unnoticed. This kind of circular reasoning dominated much of the criticism of the case; it was based upon the a priori assumption that supernormal physical events cannot occur. There are people alive today who cannot speak about the case for five minutes without becoming furious. We must look at the recorded phenomena as objectively as possible, beating the narrow path between the bigots and the zealots.

One of the wonders performed by Walter was related to readers of the *Journal* in 1932 by Button under the unhappy title: "Demonstration of the Passage of Matter through Matter: The Results of Professor Zöllner Confirmed." (Zöllner was an investigator of the confessedly fraudulent medium Henry Slade in the 1870s. By 1932, however, everyone should have known that the Slade-Zöllner investigation had been found wanting. Twenty-five years earlier, Carrington had disposed of any claim to belief in Zöllner's naïve report.) Now Button felt that the much-maligned Zöllner had been vindicated because Margery, too, had passed matter through matter using a box of Button's invention.

Certainly one of the most suspenseful ventures the Lime Street circle ever undertook was begun in March 1932, even while Dudley was examining his startling discoveries concerning Walter's remarkable thumb. Had this experiment succeeded, the society would have at last possessed evidence of an occurrence that would be self-evidently supernormal—an event that by its very nature could not be fraudulent. Walter announced one evening that he was going to try to obtain wax impressions of the foot of an unborn baby! The hot water was dutifully placed in its pan next to the cold one on the table before Margery. The hardened mass of Kerr wax was placed nearby, and everyone joined hands in the customary circle. Mina, bathed in the unearthly red light of the seance room, leaned back in her chair and, with a parting wisecrack, slowly composed herself to trance.

Walter soon came, and before long, after many of the usual complaints about the heat of the water and the difficulties under which he worked, he ordered the light, faint though it was, to be turned off. Then, in the pitch darkness, the water was heard to splash several times: first as the wax was softened and removed from the hot water, then again as it was hardened in the cold water. Two prints—undoubtedly the impressions of a baby's feet —were obtained. And Walter further informed the circle that the names of the parents of these as yet unborn babies would be forthcoming.

In later trance messages, the names were received and the entire interested world remained in suspense until the children should be born. The suspense, one need hardly add, was shared by Margery. She was indeed in a pretty fix now: the prints *had* to be genuine. There was no way that she could arrange the outcome of this little adventure merely by being nice to her friends on the ASPR research committee. Mrs. Garrett told me of receiving a phone call from Mina at this juncture, asking for advice.

Late in 1932, readers of the *Journal* were disappointed to read that the parents of one of the children refused to cooperate with the society's earnest scientific inquiries and that the other baby's print was too unclear to allow a positive identification, eliminating Walter's most exciting test from the believers' catalogue of successes.[1]

Years later, someone made the ghastly suggestion that these prints actually *were* those of babies' feet, dismembered by Crandon from the many fetal corpses available to any surgeon connected with a large hospital. The suggestion did not specifically apply to this episode, but we otherwise must account for the appearance of two fetal skin impressions made in wax in Margery's seance room; the possibility that the doctor "could sneak such things out of the hospital" was not one to be overlooked.[2]

In spite of this scandal and the nearly simultaneous announcement of E. E. Dudley's discovery, Margery's circle of believers stood firm and defended her against all attacks. One of her admirers was the Irish poet, William Butler Yeats, who was lecturing in America at this time. Crandon was Yeats's Boston doctor during his frequent visits, and their friendship seems to have been fairly close.

The late Joseph Hone's work, *W. B. Yeats, 1865–1939*, is typical of the prevailing belief among students of Yeats's life. Speaking of the poet's growing involvement with psychical research, Hone wrote, "This movement of his imagination was encouraged greatly by an encounter, while he was in Boston in 1911, with a very remarkable American medium, the wife of a doctor named Crandon" (p. 281).

But Yeats *did* know Margery in 1932, at which time he was treated to a display of psychic energy that was once again drawn from a model by Professor Zöllner. Margery (with Walter's help, of course) began the seance with two whole wooden rings lying on the table, and ended the evening's chat with her cheerful brother by displaying the two rings interlocked *but still whole and unbroken!*

Crandon thought that two of these interlocked rings should be sent to Sir Oliver Lodge for independent verification. Now it was well known that such rings could be made by carving them from the same piece of wood, but if the rings were made of different pieces of wood, there was no way to link them without breaking them. Sir Oliver dutifully received his parcel from the Crandons, opened it, and was dismayed to discover that one of the rings had been cracked and broken, presumably in transit. The remains were made of different woods, just as Walter promised. Once again fate deprived us of what could have been a striking demonstration of psychic power.

Richardson's manuscript tells of sittings given an unnamed European "literary man" recommended to the Crandons by Sir Oliver, but does not fix them in time. They probably occurred in the thirties, when Mina was beginning to tire of her unnerving avocation. This European visitor had had an unfortunate effect on Margery's spirits; her depression could only be relieved by his departure. The visitor regretfully took his leave, apologizing for the embarrassing situation. Shortly after, a personality calling itself Lila Lee took possession of Mina's motor functions. The astonished sitters then learned that Lila Lee was the deceased love of the European guest, and that she had committed suicide by throwing herself from an ombibus. She now alarmed the circle by promising to do the same to Mina. The rest is told in Richardson's own words:

We were trying in every way to calm this troubled "spirit" when, suddenly, Margery arose, and before we could prevent her, rushed down the hall and climbed a ladder to the roof of the house. She was followed closely by Mrs. Richardson, who found her close to the parapet four stories above the street. Her attitude was one of defiance. She said, "How dare you come up here?" In the presence of impending disaster Mrs. Richardson had an impulse to repeat the Lord's Prayer. Immediately Margery relaxed, and went back to the seance-room without hesitation.[3]

After this harrowing and dramatic experience, Lila Lee disappeared forever from Lime Street, but the significance of her brief appearance cannot be overlooked: the constant pressures under which Mina had lived for ten years were not without their effects on her personality.

In 1933 Brackett Thorogood published a modest apologia for Margery and the ASPR's style of psychical research, providing the case's one clear-cut experimental study that has never been explained. It was conducted to test the independence of Walter's voice from Mina's.

First, Thorogood placed a microphone in a soundproof box and locked and sealed the lid. Then he ran the cord from the microphone downstairs to the sitting room, where a speaker was set up. Returning to the fourth floor, Thorogood sat down with Mina and verified the fact that the microphone did not carry his voice to the witnesses he had stationed in the sitting room. Placing Margery under strict control, Thorogood switched off the lights and the seance began. At the end of the seance, the observers in the sitting room reported hearing Walter's characteristic voice distinctly. It had not been heard at all in the seance room. Thorogood concluded that Walter's ectoplasmic voice-box had materialized within the locked container.

Whatever strength this puzzling phenomenon gave to the case was in considerable measure diminished by several photographs in the same volume. Catalogued as Figures 74, 75, 79, and 79A, these remarkable flash photographs of Walter's hands provide nearly conclusive evidence of fraud by collusion. Figure 74 is a detail of Figure 75, and both of them show a perfectly normal masculine left hand extending from the cabinet's curtains just behind Margery's right ear. The hand is holding a small table, and, unlike earlier materializations, it seems unattached to the medium's body. It bears no resemblance to the misshapen, claw-like appendages usually claimed by Walter, but appears to be a normal hand, with normal fingers and nails, and the amount of hair usually found on masculine forearms.

In short, Thorogood's plea that this is a supernormal appendage must be entertained with due reserve. The caption beneath Figure 75 reads: "This shows the writer holding the medium's hands. Her feet are on the floor and are obviously not being used to produce this left arm. It may naturally be claimed that someone was behind the curtain, but only Adams, who was at the camera, 'Margery' and the writer were present in the locked and searched seance room. This photograph was taken Nov. 13, 1931." This photograph, despite Thorogood's claims, furnishes inescapable evidence of an accomplice in the seance room on this occasion.

Other phenomena occupying Margery's mind were of less interest. In 1932 a pharmacist named Minthorn mailed a cake of plaster with several objects imbedded in it for Walter to discern clairvoyantly. The plaster apparently was not marked to prevent substitution. By the end of 1934, Walter named its contents.[4] Skeptics suggested that Walter's task would have been easier if there were X-ray machines in spiritland—but perhaps he could use the one in Crandon's office.

Crandon claimed that Walter had extracted a chemist's vial from the plaster cake without breaking it. The unmarked cake was then mailed to Minthorn along with the vial and a list of items Walter said were imbedded in the cake. After two years, his memory might have failed, and he could have been fooled by a duplicate made from a mold of the first cake in which the objects had been imbedded in the original positions as verified by an X-ray photograph. But Minthorn was satisfied; he was attempting to impress a group of Spiritualists in his city and felt certain that this test would do the trick. The "experiment" was very weak but believers were quite impressed.

The last major disruption in the ASPR's ranks stemmed from the discontent of the zealous Frederick Bligh Bond. In May 1935, Bond allowed an editorial to appear stating his now-adverse position, followed by a summary of Cummins's findings. The statement was published without the customary review of the Publications Committee.

Pursuant to an influentially signed request on the part of Voting Members of the A.S.P.R., the Editor in this issue presents a summary of the Report of Professor Harold Cummins upon the wax impressions of the "Walter" thumbprints which have been in the possession of several English psychical researchers since the date of their original production. As these impressions in wax were in each case directly presented to the persons holding them, as sitters at the seances, and have since remained in their personal custody, it follows that there can be no possible suggestion that they have been tampered with or falsified by substitution.

It will be observed that the Report in question, which appears in the April *Proceedings of the Society for Psychical Research* (London) (Part 139. Vol xliii.) affirms in a conclusive manner the identity of the alleged "Walter" prints, specifically in all these eight cases, with the thumbprints of the living Dr. "Kerwin." The findings of Professor Cummins, a qualified dermatologist, will be generally accepted as final, and relief will be felt at the termination of a tedious and painful controversy which has not only taxed the patience of critics for a long time past, but has done injury to the cause of psychic research and harm to the repute of the very mediumship it was designed to defend.

The findings of Professor Cummins relate purely to the question of the specimens submitted to him for comparative study without any reference to a seance origin. The question therefore of their claim to a supernormal nature does not arise. The facts which he is asked to ascertain are simply whether two sets of specimens submitted are, or are not, of identical origin. Thus he remains entirely outside the area of controversy, as a dispassionate judge of the evidences submitted.

His conclusions, however, bring out in strong light the unfortunate error which led the writers in Vol. xxii of the *Proceedings of the American Society for Psychical Research* (1933) to attach responsibility for certain substitution, confusions, or falsification of evidence to Mr. E. E. Dudley, the research officer who was in charge of the seance proceedings at Boston when the wax impressions were first obtained (July 1926) and for a long time afterwards.

Mr. Dudley stands completely vindicated by the Report, and it is but right that the Journal of the A.S.P.R., as its representative organ, should declare this in no uncertain manner, and without hesitation or delay. It only remains to express the hope that the final clearance of a vexed issue which has disturbed the whole world of Psychic Research may clear the way for a further development of the constructive work of the American Society.[5]

Button's surprise may be imagined when his eyes fell on these words. He soon received and made several confused but energetic phone calls, and held a conference of the research committee to determine a course of action. Within days, a supplement to the May *Journal,* written by Button, was sent to all members of the society. The issue reached such a heated stage that the whole affair exploded onto the front page of the *New York Times* on May 13, 1935:

PSYCHICS IN ROW ON 'SPIRIT PRINTS'

Society Dismisses Editor for Questioning Genuineness of Walter Case Phenomena

TRUSTEES BACK MEDIUM

American Group's Heads Issue Apology on 'Conspiracy'—Legal Action Is Hinted

Controversy over the authenticity of spirit contacts claimed by Margery, famous Boston medium, reached yesterday a more bitter stage than ever when the trustees of the American Society for Psychical Research repudiated a statement in the May issue of its journal that purported to indicate the organization had changed its mind and now condemned Margery.

The trustees announced they had dismissed the Rev. Frederick Bligh Bond* as editor of the journal and as an employee. Mr. Bond took the news calmly. He said he had expected something of the sort and he intimated possible resort to "external authority."

A statement by the trustees is to be printed today as a special supplement to the May issue of the journal. It was composed by William H. Button, an attorney and president of the society, and by Daniel Day Walton, vice president and counsel to the organization. Both said the society, through its trustees, still held that the phenomena ascribed to Margery had been proved definitely to have been "supernatural." . . .

The statement of the trustees "apologized" and said that the society, its members and the public "have been victimized by a conspiracy to procure a fraudulent publication of the views of the society." It was declared that, contrary to orders on all matters pertaining to the Marg-

*Bond was ordained, according to Professor Kenawell's research, as "The Right Reverend Monsignor Bond, Vicar General of the Old Catholic Church in America" some time in 1932. This was, of course, a mere sect and not in any way connected with the Church of Rome.

ery controversy, the editor had failed to submit copy to the executive committee of the trustees and that the May issue had been hurried through with the officers and trustees unaware of its contents.

In announcing Mr. Bond's dismissal the trustees said that, in addition, "other avenues of redress to the society are being considered."

Mr. Bond wrote Mr. Button last Wednesday [May 8] recalling that he had given warning of an impending publication in London that would harm the organization and that he had sought authority to "forestall this by a publication of our own which would protect legitimate interests by a frank disclaimer of the unscientific and incompetent elements in the research." He went on to say that he now had published what he previously had advised.

"This I have done as a moral duty and without regard to any personal consequences," he added. "I do not propose to enter into any argument in defense of my position. I am not proposing to resign my office of editor. It is open to you, as president, either to endorse my action or to use such prerogative powers as you may possess to dismiss me if you can find lawful grounds."

Mr. Bond enclosed a copy of a letter from seven members of the society urging the journal to publish a summary of the facts of "the alleged Walter thumbprints." This letter said the Cummins report constituted "an indictment of the methods and competence of the investigation" conducted by the society's committee.

Before receiving news of his dismissal Mr. Bond said at his home at 39A Gramercy Park North that the policy of the trustees was ruled by a group "more or less pledged to support of a particular interest, namely, the mediumship of Mrs. Crandon and the advocacy of its supernormal character."

On May 14 the same paper added these details:

When Mr. Bond reached his office at 15 Lexington Avenue yesterday, he was met by Thomas H. Pierson, a trustee and secretary of the society, who handed him a letter of dismissal. While Mr. Bond was packing his belongings, the men engaged in a sharp exchange.

"I have been fired, true enough," Mr. Bond said last evening, "but the fight is on and will come out now in the open. I stand on my position.

The Margery thumbprint was trickery."

William H. Button, president of the society, maintains that the Boston medium has given abundant evidence of having supernormal powers. He is supported by a number of trustees. The controversy over the prints, which developed a few years ago, has reached a stage where the organization of more than 800 members is threatened with a split as a result of the article written by Mr. Bond.

The turmoil was quelled, however, and Bond departed peacefully, leaving Arthur Goadby, a one-time believer who now supported Dudley, to read the following at the annual meeting of the society in January:

As it has been alleged that in publishing on my own responsibility as Editor, a reprint of Dr. Harold Cummins's Report of the "Walter"-Kerwin Thumbprints I had acted disloyally to the Board of Trustees, I desire to state that my loyalty was to Dr. Hyslop's Foundation and its purposes, and that I had ceased to recognize [that] a group of persons who had usurped control of the Foundation and its endowment and had packed the Board with their own nominees and for their own purposes, in any way represented the original intention of the Founder. I considered their policy and methods to be in several ways dishonest and I knew that they had for some time past systematically suppressed the truth as to evidence in the case.

Their dismissal of Mr. J. M. Bird in 1929–30 was a warning to them that they would, if I did not submit to their policy and direction, study to discover "cause" for my dismissal, and that if I permitted them to do this, I should have served the cause of science and truth very ill.

On three separate occasions attempts were made by Mr. W. H. Button and Mrs. Crandon and by both together, to cajole or persuade me into active participation in defence of the Margery mediumship. To these suggestions I was only able to give the assurance that I would see fair play. My offer of an independent investigation into the mediumship was declined and the proposal for an independent committee repudiated.

I invited Mr. Button to allow the Journal to publish the findings of Dr. Cummins in advance of the English SPR, and so save the reputation of the American Society; but he was deaf to the offer. I therefore consider that I have taken the only right and equitable course in defending Psychic Research against an unethical and degeneratic policy which should be repudiated by all right thinking people.

I trust that the present board will realize that their conduct of this case has blasted the reputation of the ASPR as a serious scientific body and that they will see the necessity of resignation.[6]

The uproar one might have expected failed to occur, and things continued to roll downhill. The year 1936 passed in relative quiet; 1937 brought Crandon's retirement from active medical practice.

In June 1937 Mina was much heavier and looked older than she was. But Mrs. Virginia Pierson, the only witness who published an account of a Margery seance during this time, wrote: "The impression that we received in general was that the manifestations are in many respects stronger and more arresting than ever. The 'Walter' voice is deeper and more vibrant and the trance condition quickly and easily attained except when, as occasionally happens, no trance seems possible and a blank sitting ensues. Even under this disappointing condition the 'Walter' voice usually speaks."[7]

During eight seances that summer, Mrs. Pierson observed many of the usual phenomena and one interesting innovation: "On the table had been placed a china vegetable dish about eight inches long by six inches wide and in it were placed four solid red rubber balls striped with broad bands of luminous paint." In the dark, the balls could be observed to rotate within this dish while Margery was under tactual control.[8]

With the 1937 publication of the first volume of the *Journal of Parapsychology*, a new era of psychical research began. Published by Duke University, the *Journal of Parapsychology* consisted of careful, well-ordered reports of experimental studies conducted by J. B. Rhine and others on the staff of the Duke department of psychology. They were unparalleled for their success as well as for the care displayed by professional psychologists and statisticians. The methods Rhine and his coworkers used are now well known: subjects were asked to guess the order of preshuffled decks of cards and these responses were compared with the probable score to be expected by chance alone. Simple as it sounds, the results were as dramatic as any obtained in the darkened seance room, and considerably more scientific. With the conditions perfectly amenable to safeguards against fraud, these experiments provided evidence in favor of extrasensory perception more significant than all the years spent in darkened parlors and seance rooms of professional mediums.

Gradually, over a period of years, the remarkable findings published in the *Journal of Parapsychology* brought the reputation of psychical research to new heights. The ASPR greeted these important studies with only moderate enthusiasm. The memory of the 1927 hassle with Rhine was still fresh. It would not do to accord too much respect to one who had found against Margery in so decisive a manner.

Margery was therefore galled into reviving her old tests in card reading. This time she performed with a new twist: she guessed the order of the cards in an ordinary playing deck held by Fred Adler sitting ten feet away.[9] Seven such tests were recorded in December 1937, with Button present, straining his critical faculties in an effort to eliminate fraud. He neglected to separate Adler (one of Mina's oldest friends) from her by even so much as a curtain, thus failing to rule out a visual code by which Adler could signal Margery. With these "tests" (and others done the previous May in which Sary Litzelmann had correctly called 46 of 52 playing cards[10]) the society felt confident in speaking down to Rhine's less dramatic results, all of them obtained under more careful controls than ever were seen at Lime Street.

The bluff must have worked; nearly every issue of the *Journal*, by now a general potpourri of occult vagaries, contained an article on Margery's "experiments" in thought-transference. One such test in which Margery scored a hundred percent found its way into *Time* magazine in 1938; the article intimated that Rhine's findings were somehow more suspect than Button's.

Two days after Christmas, in 1939, Le Roi Goddard Crandon died in his bed after a long illness, "induced," Richardson tells us, "by a severe accident [falling down a flight of stairs] and . . . borne by him with uncomplaining courage."[11] With him died many of the secrets of the mediumship and all of the secrets that propagated it in the face of nearly continuous adversity. That grim, mysterious, intellectual face—beneath which glowed the fires of fanaticism—had dominated and directed the mediumship since its very beginning. Now that face was still; now all his questions were to be answered.

Mina's life after her husband's death became more and more disordered. It soon became apparent to her friends that she was becoming an alcoholic.

As early as 1927, she had complained that Prince was attempting to defame her by telling friends that she drank. Prince had recorded this rumor on the list of unfounded accusations leveled at him and the BSPR by the Crandon advocates (undated document, c. 1927, in Prince file). Was the rumor intended to enlist the sympathies of uncommitted observers or to cover up her actual propensity for alcohol? Liquor could be obtained easily enough during Prohibition, and with the ratification of the Twenty-first Amendment in 1933 it became commonplace. Certainly she had ample reason to drink excessively. With hordes of admirers pleading for physical proof to fortify a faith they could not otherwise maintain; with tons of paper expended in a vituperative controversy, in which Mina's innermost secrets were subject to popular speculation; with defender after defender falling from the ranks and joining the opposition; and with her own energies drained by the constant need for unparalled phenomena, it is no wonder that she turned to liquor. With no one to depend on, no one to confide in, Mina began, very suddenly, to grow old.

One of our last glimpses of Margery comes from a beautiful and sensitive article by Francis Russell in a 1959 issue of *Horizon*. Russell's only sitting with Margery occurred in 1940, on a stormy autumn evening. Standing on the stoop with their shoulders bent against the downpour, the small party waited as one of them rang the bell. Margery herself came to the door and invited them in. The light from the hallway lit her features. Little remained of the lovely and delicate woman who, sixteen years before, had laughed happily at the return of her favorite brother in the mysterious half-light of the seance room. "She was," Russell remarked, "an overdressed, dumpy little woman, amiable, yet with a faint elusive coarseness about her that one sensed as soon as she spoke."[12]

Richardson was in charge of the proceedings. The aim of the sitting that night was to obtain wax impressions of Crandon's spirit fingers. As Margery composed herself to trance, Russell was alarmed to hear her breathing deepen into "a stertorous moan." He added, "Only once before had I hears such sounds —when I passed a hospital room where a man was dying."[13]

Walter whistled shrilly in the dark and then spoke. It was "a man's voice talking very fast." Russell located the voice "several feet above Margery's head."[14] After dispensing a few satiric jabs at the sitters, Walter related disappointing news. Roy wasn't ready yet to come up with a thumbprint and everyone was to hold his horses. With a few more bantering remarks, Walter departed.

The lights were switched on. Russell had seen none of the spectacular phenomena that had captured public attention a decade before. Only Walter's voice had manifested, and that, Russell felt, was strikingly like Margery's, only "pitched in another key."[15]

Then,

Margery smiled at us in an indolent good-natured way, stretching her plump arms and yawning. As we left she shook hands with each of us at the top of the landing. "You must all come to tea next Sunday," she said. "I have a feeling it's going to be important. All of you, next Sunday— but not before five o'clock. I have to see about Roy's grave earlier." She giggled. "The landscape gardeners have made an awful mess of it, planted hydrangeas. Roy hates hydrangeas. Now don't forget—next Sunday at five."[16]

Even Richardson became estranged from Margery at the end of her life, as a result of "an action of mine which she, mistakenly, regarded as 'desertion' by one of her oldest friends."[17] This vague allusion was made clearer by Richardson's daughter, who suggested that the estrangement may have occurred when her father voiced his concern for Mina's health and his disapproval of her increasing reliance upon alcohol.

Indeed, Dr. Nandor Fodor, the unorthodox Hungarian psychoanalyst who remained Mina's friend through these difficult times, remarked upon this curious fact:

Physical mediums, in the course of years, find themselves so much drained of vital energies that almost invariably they become chronic alcoholics or dope addicts.

Not even Stainton Moses, whose honesty and probity never were questioned, escaped this fate. Margery drank herself to death. I attended many of her alcoholic seances with W. H. Button and found them pitiful.[18]

On November 1, 1941, Mina Stinson Crandon died in her sleep from complications of her chronic alcoholism; she was fifty-four years old.

She died without reconciling with Richardson, who said of her last years, "Unhappy and disillusioned as to value of her lifework, she was pursued first by Dr. Crandon's long illness and then by her own. . . . But Margery was wrong. Her fame has spread to all corners of the earth, and the facts, astounding in their nature brought out through her and Walter, are bound to have an epoch-making influence upon the physical and spiritual thought of the future."[19]

A few years later, the cheerful old doctor made his peace with Margery, who urged him to write his book. For, he wrote, "Since Margery's 'passing' I have been in what I consider most evidential touch with her through Mrs. B——, a friend of recent years . . . who possesses marked subjective psychic power. . . . Margery's only and characteristic injunction is to make it 'snappy.' "[20]

He completed his book shortly before his own death. In the closing pages he left us with the poignant hope that underlay his philosophy: "We cannot believe," he wrote, "that, in this universe of law and order, the Margery mediumship occurred without a distinct purpose."[21]

Margery's death released psychical research in America from a throttling grasp. It was followed by the retirement of William H. Button, who died three years later, and by the return of George H. Hyslop to the guiding position of the American society. He served as the society's president from 1941 until 1962, reviving serious psychical studies from the amateurish torpor in which they had languished during the years dominated by the dewy-eyed methodology and fanciful conclusions of the Margery believers.

These men and women were, in the main, lawyers, businessmen, physicians and their spouses; they vouched for phenomena which, if true, would alter the basic conceptions of science, and did so as though these things were facts which only the bigotry and bias of established science kept from general recognition.

To have had all that outpouring of supernormal energy so clumsily studied seems a prospect not to be borne with cheer. There were some things, however, which did seem—and still do seem—inexplicable. We may never know anything more about that table that chased Caldwell about the house during the very early days of the mediumship; we may never really understand how those ball bearings rolled up the ramp of the "Sisyphus" in red light; we certainly will never have the answer to the problem of the direct voice; nor were all the wax impressions so evidently fraudulent as the Walter-Kerwin thumb—we will probably never know everything about those prints of entire human palms that bore the thumbprint of another man. There were countless other questions that critics were never able to answer convincingly, but at the same time we have examined the evidence of fraud provided by such a diverse array of personalities as McDougall, Prince, Helson, Houdini, Dingwall, Hoagland, Code, Shapley, McComas, Wood, Dunlap, Rhine, Bird, and Dudley. No one could say that all these men formed a vast conspiracy to suppress phenomena that were really quite genuine. Indeed, we have seen that several of these people were firm believers in some of Mina's psychic effects at one time, only to alter their opinions under the various circumstances we have described.

We are therefore faced with three possibilities: (1) Margery was entirely genuine; (2) Margery was entirely fradulent; (3) Margery represented a case of so-called "mixed" mediumship, exhibiting features of both categories. We are armed with positive evidence of fraud in some instances at the same time that we have only possibilities of genuinesness in others. In other words, of the first two propositions, the second is immeasurably stronger than the first.

The third proposition—that the mediumship was "mixed"— provides us with that measure of safety always afforded by straddling the fence. The main argument for it acknowledges first, of course, the occurrence of fraud upon occasion, i.e., merely to "help out" the genuine phenomena; but it also clearly supposes that there were *some* truly supernormal events in the Lime Street seance room. Bird seems to have believed this when he left the society, and Bond, after his own dismissal, continued to speak of the reality of some of the phenomena, particularly the subjective material. At the same time that this position is the safest, it is also the least satisfying. One can point to no single test done with Walter that confirms the supernormal hypothesis. There is no irrefutable evidence to support the suggestion of even occasional genuineness. I have read no argument in support of this proposition that impresses me as being anything other than a personal preference.

The reader is left to make his own choice among the three propositions, although I would suggest that the first position seems untenable in view of the preceding discussion. Otherwise, since one cannot prove the universal employment of trickery, one is left to decide between the latter two with perfect freedom. The reader may here have cause to recall, as he ponders this incredibly involuted problem, Johnson's words in *Rasselas:* "Inconsistencies cannot both be right, but, imputed to man, they may both be true."

Following the long and dramatic encounter between this resourceful and fascinating woman and the forces of science, American parapsychology turned its focus away from the problems of mediumship for nearly thirty years, in order to concentrate on the basic modes of extrasensory communication. Today, with this background behind them, parapsychologists are once again investigating the fruitfulness of survival research, this time with a clearer knowledge of the problems to be overcome in approaching this, the greatest of man's mysteries.

What might have happened to modern parapsychology, had the trend begun by the fervent believers been allowed to continue, is a speculation beyond our less than oracular powers. But it was a colorful and even scandalous story while it lasted. The life of Mina Crandon was both happy and absurd; her mediumship both puzzling and disastrous. Toward the end, drink and disappointment robbed her of her youthful vitality, of her elusive gaiety, of her exuberant charm. She was only an echo of that girl who had begun that warm spring evening, seventeen years before, to shake the foundations of the world. Science and religion had reeled briefly before the incredible Margery the medium.

Now it was over.

Epilogue

THERE IS A STORY told about Margery that somehow captures the mystery, the humor, and the tragedy of her life in a way that only a myth can do. I heard it from Mrs. Garrett, and she got it from Nandor Fodor; I like to believe it is true.

In the last lingering days of Mina's life, she lay abed in a gloomy corner of her bedroom. Sitting at her side in a wooden chair was Nandor Fodor, in his hands a pad of paper. Leaning over close to the woman's face, he told her that now was the time to make a clean breast of it; both knew that she had not long to live and he suggested that she would depart happier should she dictate a confession to him. Everyone knew, he added, that *some* of the phenomena were genuine; but what methods did she use to effect the rest? How did she do it? And, most puzzling of all, *why* did she give her life for it? What had driven her to the voice in the dark? Fodor asked all the questions we have asked here; she knew she could trust him to withhold any information she might give him until after her death.

The plump face was sunk deep in a feather pillow. The once-golden curls were now faded into an indistinct shade as they rested upon the white pillowcase. She listened quietly. Then, in a weak voice, she muttered something Fodor could not understand. He asked her to repeat it.

"Sure," she said, this time more distinctly. "I said you could go to hell. All you 'psychic researchers' can go to hell."

And then Fodor seemed to see something very like the old familiar twinkle of merriment enter her eyes as she looked at him and chuckled softly. "Why don't you guess?" she said, and chuckled again. "You'll all be guessing . . . for the rest of your lives."

Notes

INTRODUCTION

1. See H. Feigl, "The 'Mental' and the 'Physical,' " in H. Feigl, M. Scriven, and G. Maxwell, eds., *Minnesota Studies in the Philosophy of Science*, II (Minneapolis: University of Minnesota Press, 1958), pp. 370–497.

CHAPTER I

1. Mark W. Richardson, "Truth and the Margery Mediumship" (Unpublished, ca. 1947), p. 89.
2. Ibid., p. 105.
3. Eric J. Dingwall, "Report on a Series of Sittings with the Medium Margery," *Proceedings of the Society for Psychical Research*, XXXVI (1928), 81.
4. Richardson, p. 89.
5. *Journal of the American Society for Psychical Research*, 23 (1928), p. 304.
6. *Journal ASPR*, 26 (1931), p. 60
7. Richardson, p. 15.
8. Ibid., p. 14.
9. J. Malcolm Bird, *"Margery" the Medium*, p. 14.
10. Dingwall, p. 81.
11. John T. Flynn, "The Witch of Beacon Hill: An Interview with 'Margery,' ", p. 7.
12. Ibid., p. 7.
13. Richardson, p. 15.
14. Dingwall, p. 81.
15. Bird, *M. M.*, p. 13.
16. Bird *M.M.*, p. 13.

17. William L. Gresham, *Houdini: The Man Who Walked Through Walls*, p. 245
18. *New York Times*, November 2, 1941.

CHAPTER II

1. J. Malcolm Bird, *The "Margery" Mediumship* (New York, 1926–1927).
2. William L. Gresham, *Houdini: The Man Who Walked through Walls*, p. 245.
3. Eric J. Dingwall, "Report on a Series of Sittings with the Medium Margery," p. 128.
4. Hamlin Garland, *Forty Years of Psychic Research*, p. 293.
5. *New York Times*, December 28, 1939.
6. Richardson, p. 106.
7. S. Ralph Harlow, *A Life after Death*, p. 72.
8. Harlow, p. 73.
9. Bird, p. 16.

CHAPTER III

1. Eric J. Dingwall, "Report on a Series of Sittings with the Medium Margery," p. 84.
2. John T. Flynn, "The Witch of Beacon Hill," p. 7–8.
3. Mark W. Richardson, "Truth and the Margery Mediumship," p. 4.
4. Ibid., p. 13.
5. Ibid.
6. Ibid.
7. Ibid., p. 13a.
8. Ibid.
9. J. Malcolm Bird, *"Margery," The Medium*, p. 16.
10. Bird, p. 20.
11. Flynn, p. 7.
12. Bird, p. 107.
13. Dingwall, pp. 86–87.
14. S. Ralph Harlow, *A Life after Death*, p. 78.
15. Flynn, p. 7.

CHAPTER IV

1. *Journal of the American Society for Psychical Research,* 28 (1934), p. 4.
2. J. Malcolm Bird, *"Margery," The Medium,* p. 22.
3. Ibid., p. 34.
4. Ibid., p. 39.
5. Ibid., p. 37.
6. Ibid., p. 40.
7. Ibid., p. 61.
8. Ibid., pp. 66–67.
9. Ibid., p. 66.
10. Ibid., pp. 66–67.
11. Ibid., p. 63.
12. Bird, p. 23.
13. Ibid., p. 48.
14. Hereward Carrington, *The Story of Psychic Science,* pp. 153–154.
15. Bird, p. 49.
16. Ibid.
17. Hamlin Garland, *Forty Years of Psychic Research,* pp. 304, 309.
18. Mark Richardson, "Truth and the Margery Mediumship," p.15.
19. T. R. Tietze, "Eusapia Palladino: A Study in Paradox," *Psychic Magazine,* 3 (February 1972, pp. 9–13 ff.; April 1972, pp. 40–45).
20. Carrington, p. 156.
21. J. T. Flynn, "The Witch of Beacon Hill," p. 8.
22. Richardson, p. 89.
23. Ibid.
24. Ibid., p. 90.
25. Ibid., p. 92.
26. Flynn, p. 42.

CHAPTER V

1. J. Malcolm Bird, *"Margery," The Medium,* p. 103.
2. Ibid., p. 51.
3. Ibid.
4. Ibid., p. 52.
5. Mark Richardson, "Truth and the Margery Mediumship," p. 104.
6. Bird, p. 90.
7. Ibid., pp. 88–91.
8. Ibid., pp. 103–106.
9. Ibid., 108.

10. Ibid., p. 111.
11. Ibid., p. 110.
12. Ibid., pp. 110–111.

CHAPTER VI

1. *Who's Who in America,* Vol. 17 (1932–33), p. 310.
2. J. Malcolm Bird, *My Psychic Adventures,* p. 112.
3. *Scientific American,* 127 (1922), p. 389.
4. Leonard Maltin, *Behind the Camera* (New York, 1971), p. 31.
5. Bird, *"Margery," The Medium,* p. 151.
6. Bird, et al., "Our Psychic Investigation," *Scientific American,* 129 (1923), p. 84.
7. Bird, *"Margery,"* pp. 404–405.
8. Bird, "Our Psychic Investigation," p. 307.
9. Arthur Conan Doyle, *Our Second American Adventure,* p. 55.
10. Walter Franklin Prince, "Review of 'My Psychic Adventures,' " *Journal of the ASPR,* 18 (1923), p. 422.
11. Bird, "Our Psychic Investigation," p. 307.
12. Ibid., p. 308.
13. Bird, "Our Psychic Investigation," p. 86.
14. Ibid.
15. Ibid., p. 71.
16. Bird, "Our Psychic Investigation," p. 14.
17. Bird, "Our Psychic Investigation," p. 379.
18. Doyle, p. 48.
19. Prince, pp. 422–433.

CHAPTER VII

1. Walter Franklin Prince, "Experiments by the Scientific American," *Journal of the American Society for Psychical Research,* 18 (1923), p. 392. Also see: Mrs. W. H. Salter, "The History of George Valiantine," p. 390.
2. Salter, p. 389.
3. J. Malcolm Bird, et al., "Our Psychic Investigation," *Scientific American,* 129 (1923), p. 14.
4. Prince, pp. 393–395.
5. Ibid., p. 396.
6. Ibid., p. 401.
7. Ibid., p. 409.

8. Bird, *"Margery," The Medium,* pp. 114–115.
9. Ibid., pp. 113–114.
10. Bird, *"Margery,"* p. 114.
11. Ibid., p. 155.
12. Hereward Carrington, *Psychic Science,* p. 201.
13. *Journal of ASPR,* 19 (1925), p. 185.
14. Ibid., p. 153. Carrington, p. 153.
15. *Journal of ASPR,* 19 (1925), p. 186.
16. William L. Gresham, *Houdini: The Man Who Walked through Walls,* p. 216.

CHAPTER VIII

1. Walter B. Gibson and Morris Young, eds., *Houdini on Magic,* p. 141.
2. Ibid., pp. 143–144.
3. Ibid., pp. 141–142.
4. Ibid., p. 156.
5. J. Malcolm Bird, *"Margery," The Medium,* p. 433.
6. Gibson and Young, p. 156.
7. Bird, p. 434.
8. William L. Gresham, *Houdini: The Man Who Walked through Walls,* p. 254.
9. Milbourne Christopher, *Houdini: The Untold Story* (New York, 1969), p. 198.
10. Gibson and Young, p. 160.
11. Ibid., p. 159.
12. Ibid., p. 160.

CHAPTER IX

1. *Scientific American,* 130 (November 1924), p. 304.
2. Grant Code, Hudson Hoagland, Everard Feilding, "Concerning Mr. Feilding's Review of Mr. Hudson Hoagland's 'Report on Sittings with Margery,' " p. 416.
3. Mark Richardson, "Truth and the Margery Mediumship," p. 101.

CHAPTER X

1. Ibid., p. 84.
2. Eric J. Dingwall, "Report on a Series of Sittings with the Medium Margery," p. 80.

3. Ibid., pp. 83–84.
4. Ibid., p. 102.
5. Ibid., p. 103.
6. Ibid., p. 125.
7. Ibid., p. 117.
8. Ibid., p. 129.
9. Ibid., p. 130.
10. Ibid., p. 129.
11. Ibid., p. 128.
12. Ibid., p. 117.
13. Ibid., p. 112.
14. Ibid., p. 116.
15. Ibid., p. 132.
16. Ibid., pp. 114–115.
17. Ibid., p. 147.
18. Ibid., p. 130.
19. Ibid., p. 135.
20. Ibid., p. 135n.
21. Ibid., p. 140.
22. G. H. Estabrooks, *Spiritism,* pp. 203–204.
23. *Journal of American Society for Psychical Research,* 19 (1925), p. 225.
24. Dingwall, p. 124.
25. Ibid., p. 140.
26. *Journal of ASPR,* 19 (1925), p. 227.
27. Dingwall, p. 140.
28. Everard Feilding, "Review: Mr. Hudson Hoagland's 'Report on Sittings with Margery,' " p. 159.
29. Dingwall, p. 156.
30. Ibid., p. 151.
31. Ibid., p. 84.
32. Ibid., pp. 157–158.
33. Estabrooks, p. 209.
34. Dingwall, p. 155.

CHAPTER XI

1. Hudson Hoagland, "Science and the Medium: The Climax of a Famous Investigation," p. 667.
2. Everard Feilding, "Review: Mr. Hudson Hoagland's 'Report on Sittings with Margery,' " p. 170.

3. John T. Flynn, "The Witch of Beacon Hill," p. 7.
4. Hoagland, pp. 669–670.
5. Ibid., p. 670.
6. J. Malcom Bird, "The Margery Mediumship I," pp. 39–40.
7. Hoagland, p. 670.
8. *New York Times*, October 22, 1926.
9. Ibid.
10. Hoagland, p. 668.
11. Ibid.
12. Ibid.
13. Ibid., p. 669.
14. Bird, p. 108.
15. Ibid., p. 35.
16. *Journal of the American Society for Psychical Research*, 19 (1925), p. 727.
17. Hoagland, p. 671.
18. Ibid., p. 673.
19. Ibid., p. 672–673.
20. Ibid., p. 674.
21. Ibid., pp. 674–675.
22. Ibid., p. 674.
23. Ibid., pp. 675–676.
24. Ibid., p. 676.
25. Ibid., p. 678.
26. Ibid.
27. Ibid.
28. Ibid., p. 678–679.
29. Ibid., p. 679.
30. Grant Code, Hudson Hoagland, Everard Feilding, "Concerning Mr. Feilding's Review of Mr. Hudson Hoagland's 'Report on Sittings with Margery,' " p. 427.
31. Ibid., p. 428.
32. Ibid.
33. Ibid., p. 429.
34. Hoagland, 681.
35. Feilding, p. 168.
36. Ibid.
37. Bird, p. 142.

CHAPTER XII

1. Ibid., pp. 287–291.
2. Ibid., pp. 292–304.
3. Ibid., pp. 312–323.
4. J. Malcolm Bird, "The Margery Mediumship I," p. 223.
5. Ibid., pp. 223–226.
6. Ibid., p. 223.
7. Ibid., p. 368.
8. Henry Clay McComas, *Ghosts I Have Talked With*, p. 18.
9. Ibid., p. 17.
10. Ibid.
11. Ibid., p. 121.
12. Ibid., p. 123.
13. Ibid., p. 124.
14. Ibid., p. 118.
15. Ibid., p. 124.
16. Ibid., p. 133.
17. Ibid., pp. 133–135.
18. Ibid., pp. 139–140.
19. Ibid., p. 140.
20. E. E. Dudley, et al., "The Margery Mediumship II," p. 718.
21. McComas, pp. 147–148.
22. Ibid., pp. 149–150.
23. Ibid., p. 145.

CHAPTER XIII

1. Carl Murchison, ed., *The Case For and Against Psychical Belief*, p. i.
2. Ibid., p. 82.
3. J. Malcolm Bird, "The Margery Mediumship I," p. 490.
4. Murchison, p. 104.
6. Ibid.
7. Ibid., p. 89.
8. Ibid., p. 91–92.
9. T. R. Tietze, "The Mysterious Wax Gloves of Franek Kluski," *Psychic Magazine*, 11 (April 1971), pp. 24–25.
10. Ibid., p. 94.
11. J. B. Rhine and L. E. Rhine, "One Evening's Observation on the Margery Mediumship," p. 411.

12. Ibid., p. 407.
13. Ibid., p. 414.
14. Ibid., pp. 413–414.
15. Ibid., p. 413.
16. Ibid., pp. 414–415.
17. Bird, pp. 4–5.
18. Rhine, p. 417.
19. Murchison, p. 95.
20. George Lawton, *The Drama of Life after Death*, p. 263.
21. Bird, pp. 229–230.
22. Rhine, p. 419.
23. Ibid.
24. Bird, p. 448.
25. Ibid.

CHAPTER XIV

1. William W. Kenawell, *The Quest at Glastonbury: A Biographical Study of Frederick Bligh Bond*, pp. 23–28.
2. Ibid., pp. 94–95.
3. Ibid., p. 98.

CHAPTER XV

1. Hamlin Garland, *Forty Years of Psychic Research*, p. 288.
2. Ibid.
3. Ibid., p. 292.
4. Ibid., p. 300
5. *Journal of the American Society for Psychical Research*, 29 (1935), p. 85.
6. Garland, p. 313.
7. Ibid.
8. Ibid., p. 293.
9. Ibid., p. 294.
10. Ibid., p. 311.
11. Ibid., p. 321.
12. *Journal of the ASPR*, 23 (1929), pp. 278–280.
13. E. E. Dudley, et al., "The Margery Mediumship II," pp. 636–642.
14. Ibid., p. 642.
15. Mrs. W. H. Salter, "The History of George Valiantine," p. 395.
16. Salter, p. 389.

17. Mark W. Richardson, "Truth and the Margery Mediumship," p. 57a.
18. Salter, p. 409.
19. *Journal of the ASPR*, 25 (1931), p. 136.
20. Ibid., pp. 139–144.
21. *Proceedings of the Society for Psychical Research*, 39 (1929–1931), p. 358–368.
22. *Journal of the ASPR*, 25 (1931), p. 143.
23. Ibid., pp. 142–143,
24. Letter from Stewart Griscom (reporter for the *Boston Herald*) to Dr. George H. Hyslop, June 18, 1927 (from the files of Walter Franklin Prince at the American Society for Psychical Research).
25. *Journal of the ASPR*, 23 (1929), pp. 295–313.
26. Ibid., pp. 270–277.
27. *Journal of the ASPR*, 24 (1930), p. 532.
28. Walter Franklin Prince, "The Case against Margery," p. 262.
29. Richardson, p. 10.

CHAPTER XVI

1. *Journal of the American Society for Psychical Research*, 26 (1932), p. 50.
2. *Journal of the ASPR*, 24 (1930), pp. 484–485.
3. *Journal of the ASPR*, 26 (1932), pp. 48–54.
4. Ibid., pp. 55–56.
5. Ibid.
6. Brackett K. Thorogood, "The Margery Mediumship III," p. x.
7. Mark W. Richardson, "Truth and the Margery Mediumship," p. 7.
8. *Journal of the ASPR*, 25 (1939), p. 147.
9. Richardson, p. 98.
10. Ibid., p. 8–9.
11. Thorogood, p. xi.
12. *Journal of the ASPR*, 26 (1932), pp. 97–132.
13. Paul Tabori, *Harry Price, The Biography of a Ghost Hunter*, pp. 163–164.
14. Ibid.
15. *Journal of the ASPR*, 25 (1931), p. 365.
16. *Journal of the ASPR*, 26 (1932), pp. 58–60.
17. Ibid., p. 46.
18. Ibid., pp. 266–276.

19. Thorogood, pp. 201–208.
20. *Bulletin of the Boston Society for Psychic Research*, 22 (April 1934), p. 26.
21. *Journal of the ASPR*, 26 (1932), p. 118.
22. William W. Kenawell, *The Quest at Glastonbury*, p. 102.
23. *Proceedings of the Society for Psychical Research*, 43 (1935), p. 17.
24. Ibid., pp. 22–23.
25. Joseph F. Rinn, *Sixty Years of Psychical Research*, p. 573.

CHAPTER XVII

1. *Journal of the American Society for Psychical Research*, 26 (1932), pp. 405–406.
2. Francis Russell, "The Witch of Beacon Hill," p. 110.
3. Mark W. Richardson, "Truth and the Margery Mediumship," pp. 81–82.
4. *Journal of the ASPR*, 29 (1935), pp. 37–51.
5. *Ibid.*, pp. 130–131.
6. William W. Kenawell, *The Quest at Glastonbury*, p. 103.
7. *Journal of the ASPR*, 31 (1937), pp. 193–194.
8. *Ibid.*, p. 194.
9. *Journal of the ASPR.*, 32 (1938), pp. 1–4.
10. *Ibid.*, pp. 65–68.
11. *Journal of the ASPR*, 34 (1940), p. 35.
12. Russell, p. 110.
13. *Ibid.*, p. 111.
14. *Ibid.*
15. *Ibid.*
16. *Ibid.*
17. Richardson, pp. 2–3.
18. Nandor Fodor, "The Coming of the Ghouls," *Fate Magazine* (March 1963), p. 45.
19. Richardson, p. 108.
20. *Ibid.*, p. 3.
21. *Ibid.*, p. 109.

Bibliography

I. BOOKS

Barrett, Sir William. *On the Threshold of the Unseen.* New York: E. P. Dutton, 1918.

Besterman, Theodore. *Some Modern Mediums.* London: Methuen and Company, 1930.

Bird, J. Malcolm. *"Margery," The Medium.* Boston: Small, Maynard, 1925.

———. *My Psychic Adventures.* London: George Allen and Unwin, 1923.

Carrington, Hereward. *The Story of Psychic Science.* London: Rider and Company, 1930.

Dingwall, Eric J. *Very Peculiar People.* New Hyde Park, N.Y.: University Books, 1962.

Doyle, Sir Arthur Conan. *Our Second American Adventure.* Boston: Little, Brown, 1924.

Estabrooks, G. H. *Spiritism.* New York: E. P. Dutton, 1947.

Garland, Hamlin. *Forty Years of Psychic Research.* New York: Macmillian, 1936.

Gibson, Walter B. and Morris N. Young, eds. *Houdini on Magic.* New York: Dover Publications, 1953.

Gresham, William L. *Houdini: The Man Who Walked through Walls.* New York: Henry Holt, 1959.

Harlow, S. Ralph. *A Life after Death.* Garden City, N.Y.: Doubleday, 1961.

Kellock, Harold. *Houdini: His Life Story,* New York: Harcourt, Brace, 1928.

Kenawell, William W. *The Quest at Glastonbury: A Biographical Study of Frederick Bligh Bond.* New York: Helix Press, 1965.

Lawton, George. *The Drama of Life after Death.* New York: Henry Holt, 1932.

McComas, Henry Clay. *Ghosts I Have Talked With*. Baltimore: Williams and Wilkins, 1935.

Murchison, Carl, ed. *The Case For and Against Psychical Belief*. Worcester, Mass.: Clark University Press, 1927.

Podmore, Frank. *Modern Spiritualism*. 2 vols. London: Methuen, 1902.

Rinn, Joseph F. *Sixty Years of Psychical Research*. New York: The Truth Seeker Company, 1950.

Tabori, Paul. *Harry Price: The Biography of a Ghost Hunter*. London: Athenaeum Press, 1950.

II. MAJOR PERIODICAL ARTICLES

Bird, J. Malcolm. "The Margery Mediumship I," *Proceedings of the American Society for Psychical Research*, 20 (1926–1927).

Code, Grant, Hudson Hoagland, and Everard Feilding. "Concerning Mr. Feilding's Review of Mr. Hudson Hoagland's 'Report on Sittings with Margery,' " *Proceedings of the Society for Psychical Research*, 36 (1928), 414–432.

Dingwall, Eric J. "Report on a Series of Sittings with the Medium Margery," *Proceedings of the Society for Psychical Research*, 36 (1928), 79–158.

Dudley, E. E. "The Margery Mediumship II," *Proceedings of the American Society for Psychical Research*, 21 (1933, dated 1926–1927).

Feilding, Everard. "Review: Mr. Hudson Hoagland's 'Report on Sittings with Margery,' " *Proceedings of the Society for Psychical Research*, 36 (June 1926), 159–170.

Flynn, John T. "The Witch of Beacon Hill: An Interview with 'Margery,' " *Collier's Magazine*, 77 (May 8, 1926), 7–8.

Hoagland, Hudson. "Science and the Medium: The Climax of a Famous Investigation," *Atlantic Monthly*, 136 (November 1925), 666–681.

Prince, Walter Franklin. "The Case against Margery," *Scientific American*, 148 (May 1933), 261–263.

Rhine, Joseph Banks, and Louisa E. Rhine. "One Evening's Observation on the Margery Mediumship," *Journal of Abnormal and Social Psychology*, 21 (1927), 401–421.

Russell, Francis. "The Witch of Beacon Hill," *Horizon*, I (3) (January 1959), 108–111.

Salter, Mrs. W. H. "The History of George Valiantine," *Proceedings of the Society for Psychical Research*, 40 (1931–1932), 389–410.

Thorogood, Brackett K. "The Margery Mediumship III," *Proceedings of the American Society for Psychical Research*, 22 (1933).

III. GENERAL PERIODICALS

Journal of the American Society for Psychical Research, 18–35 (1923–1941).
Bulletin of the Boston Society for Psychic Research, 18 (1932) and 22 (1934).
Scientific American, 128–131 (1923–1924).

73 74 75 76 77 10 9 8 7 6 5 4 3 2 1